REVERSAL
to
Renewal

A JOURNEY TO PERFECTION

By

TONYA C. EVANS

Reversal to Renewal:
A Journey to Perfection

Tonya C. Evans
Perfectly Created
tonyachelan@aol.com

ISBN 978-1-949027-73-0
Printed in the USA.
All rights reserved

Published by: Destined To Publish | Flossmoor, Illinois
www.DestinedToPublish.com

To every Believer that is wrestling with who they are as an official member of the body of Christ, who desires to live in the sweet spot where their passions collide with God's will and who wants to reverse to renew, becoming the person that God originally intended us to be - perfect. Perfectly created, that's us!

Enjoy the journey!
Lady T

ACKNOWLEDGEMENT

The path that has gotten me to this point, the writing of *Reversal to Renewal: A Journey to Perfection*, was not a straight line by any means. In fact, it has included so many twists, turns, bumps, starts, stops, doubts, denials and acceptances that it almost wasn't completed. Even while writing, I have encountered so many life occurrences that getting to completion didn't feel like it would ever happen. If it had not been for my faith, my family and my friends, there would have never been a book. This book is a true example of the rule that nothing is accomplished alone. We all need a network of people that surround us, shield us, talk truth to us, confront us, pour into us and encourage us. Therefore, I must give each one a heartfelt and sincere shout-out.

Whenever I'm asked to speak or to teach, I always give you, Keith T., a pointed and very public thank you and acknowledgement. Evans, as I affectionately call you, is my continual encourager since you and I became an *us*. When you chose me, you informed me that you were looking for a wife, someone that you could partner with in building a ministry that brings God glory by the transformation of people's lives. I'm extremely thankful for your constant encouragement and for your correction. Often, you see more in me than I see in myself. You continually add that "something special" to my life. I love being your first and only lady (yep, I just heard Freddie Jackson singing "You are my Lady" in my head too.)

Jazzy, you gave me an opportunity to see myself as being responsible for someone other than myself. Although I was married, Evans was never as dependent on me for guidance, direction and role modeling as my Jazzy. Jazzy, with your smile a carbon copy of your dad's, dimples and all, beautiful both inwardly and outwardly, with so much to give to the world, you challenged me and gave me new spaces to grow in to. Because of you I was catapulted into the next iteration of who God intended for me to become. Thank you for allowing me to be your bonus mom. I am blessed because you are a part of my life.

My Mini-Me, my Michaiah! When you burst into my life, everything changed. Just to think, I never intended to be a full-time mom, and then here you come changing everything. You have pushed (and sometimes pulled) me into becoming more of my true and authentic self. Because I have tried to live up to all of the expectations that I see in your eyes, always wanting to give you an example of what "doing it in spite of being afraid," looks like, I've gotten better, bolder and stronger. You are the fuel for my courage. My life is richer, fuller and deeper because you are in it.

Ever since I can remember, Harriet J has been the example of style and grace that I've tried to become. Never have I been able to embody your beauty, both inner and outward, but I've tried. When I was younger, all of my guy friends were in love with you and all of my girlfriends wanted to be in your space. You have always been my biggest cheerleader and you continually show up. From the moment I picked up a pen and put it to paper, for whatever reason, you have been my willing editor and critic, helping me to become a better writer and communicator. Thank you for being my mother.

Since forever, I've been told the story of how my father, affectionally known as Big Ken, promised to be all or provide all of the "firsts" in my life. The first to provide me with the significant and important things in life, the first to love, the first to protect. Although you have been all of that, you've also been the one who has given me the example of what steadfastness and being tenacious really means. How a dream never gets too old and how you never get too old to accomplish that which you've dreamed of. You've shown me that it never matters what others think. The only thing that matters is what you think of yourself. Thank you for showing me that nothing is impossible, even though it looks as if it is.

Thank you to my Greater Mt. Eagle Baptist Church family. Your acceptance has been invaluable to my growth and to the pursuit of my goals. Thank you for laughing with me and not at me. Each of you has been a part of my posse and I am extremely grateful.

My Tribe – my silent (and sometimes extremely vocal!) circle of folks that have led by example. Each of you has shown me, by the lives you live, the possibilities, the potential, how to embrace my God-given assignment and how to engage in the required work that yields powerful results. My god sisters, my friends, my Fall of 1986 sisters (Alpha Theta in the house!), my fellow First Ladies, the inner circle of the inner circle (you know who you are) and my family – this book is a result of the love and encouragement that you have always given me.

To all the women who have asked me for more, even when I did not believe I had more to give. Often, I was blind to what God had given me to give to others, but many of you saw it and you encouraged it.

To my writing coach, Deborah, thank you for hanging in here with me. I know you thought we'd never get here, to the finish line! It is because of your patience and your encouragement that I overcame my doubt, buckled down and just did it. Don't know if there will be a next, but if there is, look for a call.

To my God, my Savior and my Comforter, thank You for creating me, for giving me purpose and for giving me an assignment. Each day I live, I strive to bring You glory. You have sharpened my imperfections into a ministry that has transformed lives in ways that only You can. It is because of Your unending love, guidance, mercies and direction that I am privileged to do and achieve all that I have and all that is to come. I can never say thank You enough, but it is my prayer that I never embarrass You and that my worship is an example to the world of Your goodness, Your love and Your majesty. To You I give all honor and I give You all the glory.

I am a Christian woman who has continuously struggled with who I am, authentically, as I try to live my life in total worship of my Creator, my God. I am the wife of a pastor – commonly known in the Black Baptist Church as the First Lady (please, don't stop reading, and trust me, you'll really get something out of this). Now, if any of you are familiar with the concept of the First Lady, I'm sure you are also aware of the stereotypes that accompany that title – prim, proper, able to spit out the right scripture at the right time all the time, always perfectly appointed in dress and demeanor. She can "sang," direct the choir and play the piano – all at the same time, no less. She was born saved, sanctified and filled with the Holy Ghost and she never made a mistake at any time in her life.

Well, get ready for this. Take a seat because I can't afford for you to hurt yourself when you faint! I ain't NONE of that!

What I am is a woman who joined the church in my late teens; however, I didn't develop a real and true relationship with God until I was 25 years old. I can't sing, nor can I play the piano, so you know I don't direct the choir. Quick! Somebody get the smelling salts because I see some people going down!

Also, I've made plenty of mistakes along this path of relationship building and self-discovery. See, I was well aware of who I was outside of Christ. My continual battle is (present tense) in discovering who I am now that I am inside the body Christ and discovering who He is inside of me.

This journey has been painful, difficult, oftentimes discouraging, and filled with shame and disappointment. I've been mad at everyone – God, myself, my husband (the pastor), my parents, friends – EVERYBODY! I felt as if I was living the life of an impostor. In fact, I was the poster child for what is known as impostor syndrome – needing to be somebody or something that you don't believe you are skilled or properly prepared for! All I could see was my imperfections, my shortcomings, my being "less than" and lacking. I thought I couldn't be used by God because I was so flawed and IMPERFECT!

But, as I've studied the scriptures and continued on my journey, I've come to discover that I am PERFECTLY CREATED! God formed me in His image and likeness. Although I've been deformed by sin, I am now, by the power of my Creator, being transformed to my original state of perfection. I am PC – Perfectly Created.

So, when I teach women around the country at various churches and at women's conferences, it is my goal and purpose to reveal to them their perfection in the midst of their imperfections. To shift the lens that they are looking through and help them to see themselves as God sees them. Even though we're going through some things that seem to affirm our imperfections, we need to be exposed to how God truly sees us, and we need to start to understand that God is using each negative experience, each damaging message that we hear and play back to ourselves, each traumatic outcome to restore us to our originally perfect selves! The process is difficult, but it is definitely necessary.

Your *next*, your *greater*, is dependent on your grasping the idea of perfection! There are people who need you to help them see the perfection within and be willing to do the work to reclaim their more perfect selves.

TABLE OF CONTENTS

INTRODUCTION

"I praise you, for I am fearfully and wonderfully made.
Wonderful are your works; my soul knows it very well."
—Psalm139:14 ESV

Hello, Friend:

I know you're thinking, "Who is she to call me friend? She doesn't even know me!" You are absolutely correct; I don't know most of you (unless my family and friends are the only people to purchase this book). However, I truly believe that you chose this book because you have a need, deep down within, to better understand what the Father desires of you and who you are now that you have decided to accept the gift of salvation. How do you embrace the calling/ministry that God has for you and how do you get past the self-doubt and the feelings of inadequacy? All of the things. I've been there, done that, and I have purchased multiple souvenirs! I want to share my journey with you so that you can understand that you are not alone. This is not a space or a place of isolation. Many have traveled, and many are destined to travel, this road. You can get through this and you can live in the space of *greater*! But greater will require commitment to the reshaping of your mind and your perspective. This journey will require you to face what is true, repent, and then embrace the required change.

Listen, why wait? Let's get started!

Psalm 139 is a love letter written by David (yep, *that* David – King David, the man David!) to God about the love that God has for him, David, in spite of all his faults and shortcomings. In fact, David states boldly that he is created by God, therefore he is well made! Yep, everything that God does is done well. In fact, it's done perfectly!

Even you – you were made in perfection! Does that make you as excited as it makes me? Sit with that for a moment. Pause and take that in. You and I were made in perfection. Inhale and exhale. Inhale the idea of perfection in Christ! Exhale all of the negativity and unhelpful ideas that keep you trapped in immobility, that keep you from moving to your *next*, to your greater!

You can't see me, but I'm running right now! Running with excitement and anticipation!

David goes on to say that God continually and regularly searches him so that He can root out those sinful and unattractive parts of his character, his inner being. Look at God! Not only did He create us, but since we have been marred and deformed by sin, He still desires to remain deeply and intimately connected. He desires to develop a more meaningful relationship with us, even though we are imperfect.

It is through our imperfections that our relationship with the Creator deepens. I know, that doesn't make sense, but let me try to clear the muddy waters. Each time that God illuminates those areas of our lives, of our characters, that are not pleasing to Him and we allow Him to perform His holy surgery using trials, difficulties and tribulations to remove the unsightly parts, our faith and understanding of who He is deepens, becoming fuller and richer. More complete. Therefore, as we continue to encounter challenging situations, we begin to trust that He will provide, He will defend, He will bring us through, and that there is purpose in our going through. Our trust grows and our faith increases. Therefore, our relationship deepens.

With each surgical cut and removal, we get closer to where we started when God created us. We get closer to perfection! Thus the title of the book: *Reversal to Renewal! A Journey to Perfection.* This journey is one that will support your going back to the character, the mind and the behaviors that God intended in the beginning. We will be able to claim our birthright with boldness! What is our birthright? Everything! When God created us, He placed us as stewards over ALL that He created. Nothing is withheld from us. He expects for us to rule and to manage with confidence, assurance and power!

Why do I use "re" words? Well, *re-* as a prefix means *again*. Anytime you see *re-* in front of a word, it literally means that you have done or engaged in the root word before, and you are doing it again. For example, replay. The root word *play* means to take part in. Therefore, to replay means to take part in again. This journey will support your going back, your reversal so that you can get to perfection. You will travel through multiple *re-* words, using the lives of five Biblical women to illustrate the going back so that you may move forward. Forward to your next, forward to your greater.

Each woman will demonstrate the process and the progress to getting to your greater – to your most perfect self. Be sure to read the highlighted scriptures before reading the aligned chapter so that you can have the appropriate context. Each women will shine the light on "the how." How do we tap into the power and the character that God has for us? How do we get to the place where we can be used by Him in a special and powerful way? Your going back is for the purpose of your moving forward, and these women will help and support your journey.

Disbursed throughout the book are personal, practical and transparent moments of my own journey. I try to be open and honest about my experiences so that you can actually see that what God has for you is attainable. If I've done it, it's true: you can do it too. I share how I have grown to accept that, just like King David, I have some unattractive parts. However, in all my shortcomings, God still desires first, to have a relationship with me, and second, to use me in His program.

What is God's program? To bring Him glory and to attract others to Him. For each of us to be His Heavenly Ambassadors. Pointing others to the light and to eternal life.

I'm going to be honest; I probably will not share anything that you haven't heard or read before. I'm definitely not going to be poetic in my delivery, nor will I impress you with my vocabulary gymnastics. What I hope to do is to help you to see and to embrace the revelations of God, but in a different and unique way. I hope that this journey will help to reshape (there goes that *re-* prefix again) your mind so that you can embrace the potential and the possibilities. After embracing, I hope that you can elevate your expectations. After elevation comes engagement. Engaging in your calling with renewed (yep, I did it again) energy and commitment.

It is my desire that you no longer settle for mediocrity – just existing to exist and not contributing to the edification of the Kingdom. Friend, it is not my prayer that you are inspired, because inspiration is temporary. I pray that you are transformed. That you begin to have a renewing of your mind. A renewing that will be the springboard that catapults you to your next and to your greater.

At the end of each reading, you will find a TTT (T3): Tonya's Transformational Tidbit. This is the one thing; if you don't get anything else, be sure that you get this. The T3 will stick in your mind and give you something to think on and to chew on. T3 should support you in your transformation; as you grow, you will be able to recall the T3 and be encouraged.

At the end of each entry, I will pray with you. Praying that you are not overwhelmed, confused or feeling defeated. Praying that you are encouraged to continue and that you are energized to move forward to the next entry. Some entries will require you to take a beat and just think about what you've just read. It will force you to really look at yourself and begin to change your thinking and, ultimately, your behaviors. Behavior change takes time. So, take your time and don't rush through trying to get to the end. Be kind to yourself. This is not a race to the finish but a journey to total change. This is a mission of transformation!

So, as you reverse to go forward, please remember that you are fearfully and wondrously made. You were made to glorify God. You will glorify God by stepping into your calling with boldness, courage and confidence. Yes, God will continue to search you, He will continue to challenge you, and He will continue to confront you, but He will never leave you, nor will He forsake you. David states in Psalm 139 that he cannot hide from God. Wherever David goes, God is there! Even if those places are as unpleasant as Hell itself. God is even there. That should bring you peace.

Again, I call you friend. I call you friend because I am walking with you as you travel the roads that I have already traveled. I've been here and I've done this. I'm also continuing on the journey because it ain't over, never, ever. I want to assure you that as you embrace the work and move further on the journey, your steps will get lighter and your vision will become clearer. The ultimate goal is that you will submit your will to the will of the Father, and you will be all about operating in your sweet spot – the space where your passions collide with God's calling. As you continue, our friendship will become more apparent, because a friend is someone that will be with you even in difficult and challenging times.

Safe travels, my friend,

Lady T

T3:

You are on a journey to reclaim what God intended from the beginning – a deep and rich relationship. You are reclaiming your perfection.

PRAYER:

Dear Lord, Father God, The Creator of all good and perfect things, including me,

Thank you, Father, for directing me to begin this journey to perfection. Now, strengthen me as I move forward to reshaping my thoughts, my actions and my behaviors. Help me to move fearlessly and with commitment so that I can become a useful instrument in the building and expanding of Your kingdom. Thank you for Your loving kindness and Your desire to develop such a meaningful, rich and full relationship with me.

In Jesus' name I pray,
Amen

REDESIGNATE:

GIVE (SOMEONE OR SOMETHING) A DIFFERENT OFFICIAL NAME, DESCRIPTION OR TITLE

Hagar: Genesis 16 & 21:8 – 21

The Egyptian slave, a handmaiden of Sarah, Abraham's wife. Sarah gave Hagar to her husband, Abraham, known at the time as Abram, as a "wife" to bear him a child. Abraham's firstborn son through Hagar, Ishmael, became the originator of the Ishmaelites, generally taken to be present-day Arabs.

LIVING UPWARD

My husband & I were watching the movie *Antwone Fisher* and were extremely disturbed by the fact that Antwone was constantly being referred to by the derogatory term "nigga" by his foster mother. His foster mother was someone that was *paid* to care for and aid him to become a well-balanced and confident adult. Never did the foster mother call him by his birth name, Antwone. Nor did she use terms of endearment like sweetheart, baby, dumpling or love. Never did she attempt to build him up! She forever used deprecating references – demonstrating how little she valued or cared for him. What bothered me most was not just the use of the name, but how that name was the complete and honest description of how she treated and how she thought about him – no love, no care, just continual mental, physical and verbal abuse. As a result, as Antwone matured, that name and the maltreatment that accompanied it shaped the way he saw himself and determined how he lived out his life. He couldn't see himself as anything but the "nigga" that his foster mother saw. He couldn't love himself!

The names that others give us, how they treat and mistreat us, often impact how we see and value ourselves. We start to develop the characteristics and behaviors that demonstrate the words, titles and names that people use in reference to who we are. Sometimes those words describe our circumstances: "low income," "learning disabled," "single mother," "unemployed." Other times they describe the perception of who they say we are: "lazy," "unmotivated," "trifling," "low class," "unworthy," "helpless." With the continual barrage of such mean and corrupting words and references, we begin to personify whatever negative stereotypes and behaviors that are associated with those words.

Hagar, in Genesis 16: 1 – 2, is referenced as a handmaid, a female servant, and in some versions, she's referenced as a slave, a person who is the property of another and is forced to obey their owner. Hagar's only value was whatever her owner determined; she was obligated to perform as her owner desired.

Just like Antwone and Hagar, our circumstances and how others determine our value can cause us to live and respond based on that devaluation. We see ourselves through the lens of others. Our self-perception is clouded by the dirt that others throw at us. We can't see our true selves, the people that our God created us to be, because our minds are fixated on the negative – our circumstances, situations, unfortunate events and occurrences. We begin to allow those things to dictate who we are, therefore missing the opportunities to live the greatness that God created us for.

We were created to live as a representation of God himself to the world. We were created for GREATNESS!

Yep, before I had my epiphany moment and realized that God had created me for GREATER, I, too, lived my life based on the perceptions of others, living down to their low expectations.

Allowing them to determine who I was and how I behaved! Shoot, I expected nothing good from myself because I expected my outcomes to be equivalent to the low expectations of others. I became who THEY said I was.

It was not until I embraced, *fully*, the idea that God created me in His image and likeness that I began to live a life larger than my beliefs and the beliefs of others!

See, I found out that as long as I live boldly and powerfully in Christ, my destiny isn't determined by the names, images, stereotypes and expectations of others. It's not even determined by those things that I call myself! My value is determined by God's love for me. How He values me! Based on God's valuation, I am:

- more precious than rubies,
- more than a conqueror,
- victorious,
- His child,
- His friend,
- worthy,
- prosperous,
- chosen,
- a royal priesthood,
- His workmanship, and
- to be used for His purpose!

It doesn't matter what others say I am or who they say you are. Neither the names they have for you nor how they categorize you are of any consequence or concern! In all actuality, it doesn't matter who we say we are. What matters is that every morning, we wake up determined to see ourselves as God sees us and to then live our lives based on THAT image.

T3:

We must commit to living upward! We were created to live as a representation of God himself to the world. We were created for GREATNESS!

PRAYER:

Lord God,

Thank you for calling me Your child, beloved, a victor, a friend. It is by those names that I will operate and be defined. It is by those names, provided in love, that I will find my identity. It is in those names that I will represent You.

In Jesus' name I pray and claim victory,
Amen

VISION OF GREATNESS

When I found out that I was pregnant, I immediately began to see my child in completion. I could see my baby as an infant, as a child, as a teen and even as an adult. Before I even knew my baby's gender, I began to wonder who the baby would become. Not in terms of the baby being male or female, but who the baby would become as a human being. How could I aid my child in becoming the best version of whatever he or she was going to be? But, because of the multiple challenges I had endured that caused me to form a poor self-image, it was difficult for me to picture my child living or becoming GREAT. My vision was clouded by my pain and hurt.

Yes, I know that I should have been concentrating on the awesome possibilities that my child had before him or her. Yes, I had come a long way in reshaping my self-image and had started embracing the life that God had outlined and destined for me. However, in that moment, when I knew that I was about to give birth to a child who would have to endure the cruelties of this world and would have to make multiple mistakes along his or her life's journey, it was difficult for me to embrace the positive possibilities. Knowing that sometimes circumstances can derail you from your ultimate destiny. Knowing that trials and difficulties can skew your thinking and you begin to display the scars of your past injuries. Knowing that people are not nice and that they are not always kind. Knowing that evil and ugliness are forever present. Needless to say, I was excited because my husband and I wanted a child, but I was terribly afraid of the pain that my child wouldn't be able to avoid. Far too often, during those 40-plus weeks, I focused on the negative, on the hurt and on the potential pain.

For each of us, because our thinking is hampered by the residue of our past while we endure the difficulties of our present, it is tough for us to see God and the possibilities of what *can be*. We are surrounded by such negativity that our ability to see beyond to the better is strained. We experience an existence that is covered by cataracts – a cloudiness of our vision that prevents us from seeing the wonderful possibilities that God has created for us. We are so stuck in the lowliness of life that we can't free our minds to see beyond the obstructions, the clouds, the cataracts.

In Genesis 16, Hagar, because of the harsh treatment of her owner, tried to run –trying to relieve the pain. As her situation became too much to endure, she attempted to escape. I can hear her, as she prepared to make her run for it and even as she ran, saying, "I know I'm a slave and I have no real value. I know that I've been used as a pawn in the games of my master. I know that I am now pregnant with a child that will not be considered my own. But I can't do this anymore. My situation probably can't get any better, but I can't wait around here for it to get any worse. Because it is going to get worse! It can only get worse."

Our vision is so blurred by anguish, gloom and our own low-level thinking that we fail to see the intentions of God! We see the difficulties, we see the challenges, we see the mistreatment. We concentrate on so much negativity that we miss the greatness that God has created for us and to be created by us for others. We miss the promise because we are besieged by the hopelessness. Just like Hagar, we will need to be reminded that God has intended for you to be great! You were created and conceived for greatness! We must begin to retrain our minds to think on the goodness that our God has for us. That we were created in His image and likeness and that He has a plan to use us in the building and adding to His kingdom! Yep, better is within our power, but it requires commitment to wanting to see the potential rather than the problems! We've got to remove, with the help of God, the cataracts that are clouding our vision to the potential and the possibilities.

God has done a great work in you! Meaning, He has created you with purpose for a calling that will indicate to the world who He is. Therefore, your future is not hindered by your past. Your future is not determined by your present. Your future is determined by the love of God to be manifested through you! God created you to be a blessing to someone else.

Go be great!

T3:

With God and our embracing of His vision, we can embrace greater and see, without obstruction, the possibilities and the wonderful expectations of our Creator!

PRAYER:

Dear God,

Perform Your miraculous surgery and remove anything that obscures my vision of the greater that You have for me. Help me to see clearly Your will and Your intentions for my life.

In Jesus' name,
Amen

ENDURANCE: A REQUIREMENT

Every year, just like many of you, I have intentions of losing weight, getting stronger and developing the proverbial six-pack. I watch people on television, in magazines and on social media who seem to just instantaneously go from being overweight and out of shape to being thin, tight and looking right. With those images in mind, and having the idea that the transformation occurred overnight, every year since forever, on January 1, I pledge to live a transformed life. I select a new eating plan, join a program, get a new spa or gym membership, develop a workout plan and write down S.M.A.R.T. goals – Specific, Measurable, Achievable, Realistic and Time Bound. Yes, I'm a little anal about things sometimes! That's on January 1! By Valentine's Day, I am back to eating everything that hasn't been nailed down while sitting on my couch in the workout clothes purchased but never used for the purpose intended. As I continue to regain the small amount of lost weight and losing the small gains I've experienced in getting closer to that much-too-distant six-pack, I realize that being inspired ain't the same as being transformed. True transformation requires endurance and commitment.

Endurance: the power to sustain an unpleasant or difficult process or situation without giving up. The process is not enjoyable. In fact, the word alone indicates that some discomfort is to be expected. However, the word also forecasts, when it is connected to God and His will for our lives, that there is going to be a blessing if we just hang on and hang in.

After the Angel of the Lord told Hagar she would be the mother of a great nation, the angel told her she would have to return to Sarah – she couldn't run. She would have to bear the mistreatment in order to receive the blessings God had planned for her life and the life of her child. She would have to endure.

God does not place us in difficult situations without having an intended purpose for the difficulty. He wants us to endure so that we are adequately prepared for the blessing.

As the Apostle Paul writes in Romans 5, endurance has a purpose. That if we endure, our character will be strengthened and we will be prepared for the better that is in our future. Just like with my yearly pledge to lose weight and get healthier, it requires me to commit and to endure the process – not eating everything that I may want, using the purchased gym membership and experiencing some pain and discomfort. Why? Because it is through endurance that my mind is changed, my habits are rehabilitated and I am truly TRANSFORMED. My previous thoughts about food and exercise cannot sustain my changed image of who I am becoming! My new, improved and strengthened character.

In order for us to maintain the change that God is working in our lives, our thinking must be changed. We'll need to develop habits and behaviors that will support the newness that is within. Our minds must not continue to support the before – a life in which we were destined for less than our potential. Our minds are now required to think as our redesignated selves! The healthy and fit version of ourselves! We can only maintain our transformation if we have learned, through endurance, to behave and react differently.

To be inspired is temporary, but to be transformed requires endurance.

T3:

God does not place us in difficult situations without having an intended purpose for the difficulty. The intended blessing involves skills, talents and abilities that we must develop so that we can handle it.

PRAYER:

Dear Lord,

Help me to endure the discomfort, embrace the uneasiness and celebrate the transformation. Help me to realize that it is by this temporary discomfort that I will be transformed into an instrument that can be fully employed for Your purpose.

In Jesus' name,
Amen

OBEDIENCE IS REQUIRED

From the day my daughter was born, she has been pushing back on my authority as her parent, challenging the expectation to be obedient. Whenever I tell her to do or not to do something, she asks me why! Even as a toddler, she would look at me as if to say, "Why are you telling me to be still or to go to bed? I am not ready to do that!" That is just her nature. It is just in her to challenge my direction, suggestions or commands. Even if she knows it's for her good, she is still compelled to ask why and to challenge (I wonder where she gets that from?). It drives me CRAZY!

What led to the deformation of man, being deformed from the original image and likeness that God created us in, was disobedience. It was (and is) our need to challenge authority. We challenge because we believe that we know what is best for us. When God gave us the ability to choose, known as free will, it created multiple opportunities for us to challenge His authority in our lives. It has given us opportunities to choose to perform in the exact opposite way from what God intends.

However, I've come to learn that when we are obedient, there is a blessing. That if I had submitted my will to His will sooner, there would have been less troubles, less agony, less distress and less discomfort.

Whenever God challenges us with the need to follow and be obedient to His direction, and we actually and truly submit, there is a blessing. Now, it's not always a tangible *I can see and put my hands on it* type of blessing. Often the blessing is in the growth of our commitment to Him, the transformation of our character or the deepening of our relationship. But with all confidence, I can say that there is a blessing!

In Genesis 16: 9, the Angel of the Lord tells Hagar, the servant of Sarah and the surrogate of Abraham's child, to return to the harsh treatment of her master and to endure. WHAT? Who does that? Who willingly subjects themselves to being mistreated? You must remember, because of free will, that if she is obedient to the desires of the Creator, it is by CHOICE.

I'm sure that Hagar thought to herself that the Angel of the Lord must be aware of what she was trying to get away from, the harsh treatment that she was running from. Why would he send her back? But then comes verse 10 where the angel informs Hagar that if she returns and if she endures, then she will become the mother of many descendants. So many descendants that she will be unable to count! HUH?! By being obedient and returning to a situation that seems to be unbearable, I will be blessed to be the mother of a nation! WHOOP! THERE IT IS! THE BLESSING!

If Hagar and, ultimately, each of us, makes the intelligent choice to select God's will over her own, there is a blessing. Even if by doing so we must encounter and endure distress. By Hagar 's obedience, in addition to becoming the mother of a nation, she comes to understand several things:

1. She will survive!
2. The treatment that she will endure will not be bigger than the blessing she will receive.
3. Temporary discomfort can result in a victorious future.
4. There's a purpose to her suffering, and
5. We don't know or understand it all, therefore we must trust the One that does!

It is my prayer that each of us can have a transformative experience just like Hagar. If you continue to read chapter 16, you see that Hagar realizes that she has deepened her relationship with the Creator. She states that she has just engaged with the God that "sees her!" Seeing her means that He not only recognizes her existence but that He sees her in totality. He responds to her need and He has a plan for her. However, for her to receive the fullness of the plan, she must choose obedience!

Obedience is contrary to who we are naturally. But obedience is necessary if we want to receive the fullness of God's blessings. It may be tight, but it definitely is right!

Obedience is the key!

T3:

Whenever God challenges us with the need to follow and be obedient to His direction, and we actually and truly submit, there is a blessing.

Prayer:

Dear Lord,

Help me to be obedient to Your direction and the will that You have for my life. Help me to depend on Your insight and not only on what I can see and imagine. Our vision is finite, where Yours is infinite. Thank you for being my guide.

In the precious name of Jesus,
Amen

Our God is Intentional

As I continue my journey of redesignation, changing my destination from death to life, I have a better understanding of the intentionality of God. I must admit that my arrival to this space has not been easy and has not always been appreciated or respected by me. However, I realize that everything that I've endured has been necessary for my growth, development and preparation for the "next," whatever that next is. That God has intentionally created and orchestrated situations in my life to get me to my greater.

In the spirit of full transparency, I've had moments of doubting God's promises. Yep! I've doubted whether God is going to use me. Based on my current circumstances, is God truly going to stay with me and not leave me? Or am I that *one* child that He just can't seem to get to the place where I can be useful and effective? Has God thrown His holy hands up, decided that He could better use His energy on someone else and just left me alone? In those times, truly, I can't see God's face and I can't feel His power or His presence.

See, I have read, studied and believed God's word. However, many times my confidence is that God will and can bless anyone and everyone else. Will He bless me? I think to myself, and I often say out loud, "I've been obedient, *most of the time*, I've followed God's direction, *most of the time*, I've submitted my will to His, *most of the time*, I've done all of the things!" In the dark moments, those moments when I'm tired. When I've fought the good fight and have seemingly come up on the losing end. When I've had to engage in that recurring battle and I don't seem to be making any progress. When I've suffered one defeating blow or disappointment too many, I begin to doubt God's word as His word speaks to or about me. I start to doubt God, the plan and the process.

Just like Hagar, God has spoken to each of us and informed us that He has a plan for our lives and that the plan is meant to bring glory to His name and for us to prosper. Our prosperity and advancement are solely tied to His glory!

But in the journey, we hit some wilderness and valley experiences that will place us in a space of doubt, despair and desperation. It is in those valleys and dark moments that God will have the *plan* and His *promises* to cry out to us as a reminder of His never-ending presence and forever love for us.

In Genesis 21:17 & 18, God speaks to Hagar, as she is in one of her darkest moments, and informs her that He has heard the cries of Ishmael. It is through Ishmael that His plan will become a reality. It is through Ishmael that God will make Hagar the mother of many descendants. The plan is dying! God has heard the choking cries of His promise.

Our doubts, fears, lack of endurance and lack of commitment can potentially choke off God's plan from becoming reality.

Please notice that although Hagar is crying, God speaks to the death of the plan – HIS promised plan! He speaks to the fact that she is allowing her *right now* to cripple the promise and the things that are to come.

It is in this space and place of fear and doubt that God chooses to remind us of His presence. That His plan WILL be manifested. He reminds us that, just as Paul stated in Romans chapter 8, that everything we are experiencing is for our good. It is the necessary preparation for what is coming. This dark place has a purpose for the next portion of the journey. He reminds us that our current situation is a portion of the plan and that He has a purpose for our current madness.

He also reminds us that this is intentional. This discomfort has purpose. This space of doubt has purpose. His seeming distance has purpose! Therefore, we must lean into the process. Lean into the darkness. Lean into the pain. Leaning in with confidence in God and in His promises.

Why are we confident? Because God intentionally provides moments like these so the fullness of His plan can come to pass and so we will be FULLY prepared for the outcome. What is the outcome? That God be glorified.

T3:

Don't allow your present to cripple God's promised plan for your life. Our God is intentional, therefore we must lean in and see what glory will be the result!

PRAYER:

Father,

Help me to lean into the present so that I can move forward to the next, into the greater! Remind me to trust that You won't leave me. Even in the dark spaces, You are with me and You are purposeful in your work. My greater is dependent on Your intentional plan. Thank you, God, for Your intentionality in my growth.

In Jesus' name,
Amen

Our Journey is Just That
– Ours

My husband travels often, and one of the perks of being the First Lady is that, sometimes, I get to tag along. Many times, our travels are to attend a national conference in which many pastors and their wives from our state are attending. Once, due to some commitments, we had to leave considerably later than others attending the conference. They were leaving from the same destination, using the same airline and going to the same place, with the same goal of arriving all in one piece! Unfortunately, my husband and I experienced multiple delays. Once in the air, we had severe turbulence, and the landing was rough. We got our bags and went to pick up our rental and were informed that there weren't any more available but that they were getting some brought in from another location and they would be available in the morning. We caught a cab to the hotel; it was very late in the evening and we hadn't eaten. We tried to order room service, but the kitchen was closed. We called the front desk to get some suggestions and was informed that everything nearby was also closed. Luckily, our room had a minibar. That evening we dined on chips, soda and some chocolate that cost more than a five-course meal at a five-star restaurant. Then we went to bed, hoping that tomorrow would be a better day.

The next morning, we met up with others from our state. They asked about our flight and we commenced to inform them of our multiple trials and tribulations. They shook their heads, patted us on our backs and told us about how pleasant their day of travel was and how tasty the hotel restaurant's food was! To say that Tribe Evans was unhappy would be an understatement. Let the truth be told, we were angry! So angry that for the rest of the morning it was difficult to fully engage in the conference.

Have you ever had that type of experience? You've read the promises of God and you've heard His voice speak to you, clearly, about His intentions for your life. However, when you witness someone else's journey and compare it to your own, it doesn't seem as if they've had to endure difficulties and setbacks at the same level of stress and pain as you have. Or they seem to experience more fruit for their labor when compared to you. That your high moments just don't seem to be as high and your low moments seem to be so much lower. I know I'm not in this thing by myself.

I'm sure that Hagar had the same questions when she took a moment to compare her situation to that of Sarah's. They both were promised, Hagar directly and Sarah through Abraham, that they would be the mothers of immeasurable descendants. However, Hagar was a slave (and was treated like one), while Sarah was the respected owner of slaves. Hagar was obligated to take orders, while Sarah was privileged to give them. Hagar was forced to leave the camp, while Sarah was the owner of the camp. Almost the exact same promise but different journeys.

In both situations, the one my husband and I faced and the situation of Hagar and Sarah, the focus should be:

1. God is the giver of the promise, and He determines the journey.
2. God cannot lie, so the promise is assured.
3. If God said it, then we should believe it.
4. The ultimate goal will be accomplished, and
5. God is being glorified.

The journey is different, but the destination is the same – the glorification of our God. It doesn't mean that one journey is better or more valuable than the other. They are just different.

Don't get caught up in the comparison game! Just like my husband and I, because we were focused on comparing our journey to the journeys of the others, that morning we missed so much that God wanted to share with us and have us experience. We were so focused on the trials and the differences that we missed many opportunities to praise God for His presence in our lives and for the experience that He had provided!

T3:

Nobody's journey is better or worse than someone else's. Our journeys are our own! We must value them for what they are and praise God for it ALL.

PRAYER:

Dear God,

Thank you for the promise and for the journey. Thank you for even the bumps and bruises along the way. I must remember that it is all for Your purpose and for Your glory.

In the name of Jesus,
Amen

SOME THINGS JUST SEEM CRAZY

The last that we read about Hagar and about her son, Ishmael, is in verse 21:20, when we learn that they never returned to Abraham's home after being sent away. Rather, they remained in the wilderness, and Ishmael's skills as a warrior were perfected. Most importantly, we learn that God remained with Ishmael, even in the wilderness.

The journey of redesignation, being moved or transformed from what you are now to something totally different, is exhilarating and exacerbating, exciting and disappointing, easy to understand and difficult – all at the same time. The journey is not for the weak, but it also isn't for those who believe that by their own strength they can make it happen. Redesignation is not meant for the timid and the fearful. It requires patience, courage, boldness and FAITH.

Faith is believing, without deviation or hesitation, that what God has promised is true and that it will happen. Even though everything around you would cause anyone looking into your situation to doubt, you must know that it will happen. Your money may be funny and your change may be strange; however, you believe that when God said that you would be a lender and not a borrower, it will happen. Even though you didn't graduate from college and you are the product of a single-parent home with a meager income, you believe that you are royalty. Even though people don't know your name and you are often ignored, you believe that you are a light on a hill. Yep, if people were to look at your present situation, it would make sense that what you are believing should be doubted. Yep, it just seems too crazy and too far out of the realm of possibility to actually be true.

However, what we need to know for sure is that if we continue to walk this journey in faith, despite what seems to be obvious, God will honor His word and He will remain with us in the dark moments and in our wilderness experiences.

Just as Hagar, once a slave who was considered of little to no value, who was used and manipulated for someone else's purpose, became the mother of a great nation, your life can be one of abundance, living in the reflection of God's glory and participating in His will. Regardless of what seems obvious – your defeat, we must have faith that what God says about us is true. Yep, it may be a little crazy, but we know that God has worked with less!

Therefore, we will lean into the journey. Praise God for His love and for His desire to use us in His plan. Then we will engage in the process. Everybody won't see it, and that's fine. Some will want to remind you of what you used to be, and that's fine. Some will challenge your existence and want to distance themselves from you, and that's perfectly fine. We will resolve in ourselves to listen to the master planner and submit ourselves to the process.

T3:

Regardless of what seems obvious – your defeat, we must have faith that what God says about us is true. Others will be astounded by the outcome of your faith! But it ain't about them. It's all about HIM! In and through it all, God must get the glory!

PRAYER:

Dear Father,

You are the Master Planner, and what seems ridiculous to man is certainly possible when it is in Your hands. Therefore, I will trust You, even in the darkness. I'm faithfully walking towards You. Faithfully returning to my perfection!

In the miraculous name of Jesus,
Amen

REALIGN:

To Change One's Position or attitude

Leah: Genesis 29:16 – 35

The oldest daughter of Laban and older sister of Rachel. Jacob was tricked by Laban into marrying Leah, though Jacob was deeply in love with and hoping to marry the beautiful and attractive Rachel. Leah is the mother of six sons by Jacob: Reuben, the oldest of Jacob's children, Simeon, Levi, Judah, Issachar and Zebulun. She is also the mother of Jacob's only daughter, Dinah.

THE OPINION OF OTHERS:
PART 1

When I was a kid, there was a cartoon that I would watch every Saturday morning: *Recess*. I LOVED that cartoon. TJ, the main character, was loved by everyone. To say that he was popular is an enormous understatement. He was always the life of the party and he could always come up with the best plans to get himself and his friends out of some kind of trouble that his mischievousness probably had gotten them into. In one episode, there was this kid who did not like TJ, and he told him so. For the entire episode, TJ did everything he could to show this kid how great of a person he was, while excluding and ignoring his original friends, his true gang, those who had been with him from the beginning and already liked him for who he was. The two of them had the BEST time – playing on the playground, going through secret tunnels, visiting all of TJ's best spots! They had a blast.

At the end of the day, it was time for everyone to go home, and TJ asked the kid if he had a good time and the kid replied in the affirmative, enthusiastically! Then TJ asked the question that he really wanted answered. The question that would highlight whether or not all of his hard work had been in vain. Had he achieved his ultimate goal? His entire self-image hinged on the response to this very important question. As a kid, I sat there nervous, hands sweating and heart beating rapidly, because I could anticipate the question coming and I wanted, no I *needed*, for TJ to get the response that he was hoping for. Truth be told, I wanted the same thing that TJ wanted, to be liked by everyone that I came into contact with. So TJ asked it: "So, do you like me now?" Everything stopped for at least 10 seconds with the camara focused on TJ and then the kid, TJ and then the kid. The suspense was killing me. I mean come on, the kid HAD to finally like TJ, right? After all of the energy and effort that TJ put into the day. The kid looked TJ directly in the eyes, smiled, quickly said, "NO!" and got on the bus to go home!

WHAT?! Wait! REALLY?! So, that's how it's going to end? I was sooooo angry. I watched as TJ, obviously devastated, turned away from the bus – and who did he see waiting to greet him? His true friends, the original gang, the ones that already cared for and loved him. They loved him not because of the fun he could provide for them. They just loved him for who he was. Even though he'd ignored them for the entire day, in the end they were there for him, received him, embraced him and continued to love him in spite of himself.

Romans 5:8 NKJV says, *"But God demonstrates his own love for us in this: While we were still sinners, Christ died for us."* God, in spite of how we ignore Him and put others in front of Him, remains, and He stays closer to us than a brother. God receives us when we are ready to turn to Him, in spite of ourselves. He never leaves or forsakes us; we turn from Him to something or someone else, but He remains.

Just like TJ, we get consumed with trying to get the love and appreciation from someone whose love and/or attention is temporary or dependent on what we can give or provide. Our God doesn't push or force us to see Him. He just waits for us to come back to Him. His love is unforced, and it can't be earned. His love just is! It is because He is love and He gives it openly! He just requires us to realign our priorities to align with His. We must make pleasing God our primary goal. His opinion is the only one that matters!

T3:

God doesn't look to get anything from us other than our obedience and commitment. He is so ready to give us so much that we can't work for. We just need to put God's opinion first!

PRAYER:

Dear Lord,

How wonderful You are for loving me fully, even though I am imperfect. You love me perfectly and completely. I accept Your love and I appreciate Your perfect acceptance of my personhood.

In Jesus' name,
Amen

THE OPINION OF OTHERS: PART 2

Previously, I introduced one of my favorite cartoon characters, TJ from the cartoon *Recess*. TJ, instead of focusing on the love he already had, chased after a love that was being withheld and denied. I've been there and done that! Ever since I was a child, I've spent so much of my time and effort trying to be accepted, liked, and loved by people who were never going to love me in the first place. I've been consumed with comparing the popularity of others to mine and I've expended so much of my energy trying to increase others' adoration of me. I've watched as others were invited to parties or to tables that I was never even considered for. Listen, I can't even enumerate the number of hours I've spent, or measure the energy I've expended, showing people how much I could add to their lives, trying to get them to appreciate my value.

Often, the only thing I've gotten from my efforts is disappointment and pain. Furthering my idea of myself as not being good enough. No, I did not get the love that I was chasing and hoping for. No, I wasn't considered a source of their joy. No, I didn't get an increase in invitations to the party. No, people didn't start to say, "Hey, wait. Let's check in with Tonya to see what she thinks," or "This won't be any fun unless we include Tonya," or "WWTD, What Would Tonya Do?" What I did get was continual blows to my self-esteem. Developing an image of not ever being enough! Not good enough to be a part of their inner circle, their tribe or their group.

I must've been about 25 years old, and I was at one of the lowest points of my life. My friends were all getting married, advancing in their careers and/or having children. They seemed to be living the dream – MY DREAM! I wasn't getting married, and I didn't have any prospects with potential. I'd changed my career, which resulted in my having an extremely low-paying job at a not-for-profit organization. Surely, in all of this madness, I wasn't having anybody's children. My life was so far away from the dream that I couldn't even fathom anything better or greater. My vision was so shortsighted and hampered.

One day, during my private Bible Study, the Lord spoke to me, loudly, from His word. I was studying John 15 when I read verses 13 – 15, where Jesus explains that He has such high regard and love for me that He considers me His friend. Wait, what? As inferred by the text, there's no greater love! Jesus loves me so much that He has sacrificed His life so that I can have the benefit of all the blessings of my God and the ultimate gift of eternal life!

Once that hit my heart in just the right way and penetrated that hardened shell of low self-esteem and negative self-image, I realized that the opinions of others meant nothing. FINALLY! The light came on. My concentration and concern shifted from what was going on around me and were realigned to focus on the one that has sacrificed His life for me. It ain't about others, it's about Him!

We are so consumed with getting and receiving love from *people*. We go to great lengths to impress people who care so little about us. We pour so much of our valuable resources – our time, our talents and our emotions – into people who do not consider us vital or important. We allow people to use and misuse us in effort to get them to accept and embrace us. We are on a mission to impress people who would not be impressed by anything that we do. Yes, they'll accept the gifts we bring, but they will not give anything in return.

But God! The love that Jesus has for us is so intense and so deep that He sacrificed Himself for us and we've done nothing to get it. All that He asks is for us to make His Father, God, Number One in our lives.

T3:

Our concentration and concern must shift away from the opinion of others, and it must realign to focus on the one that has sacrificed His life for us. It ain't about others; it's all about Him! We've got to get our priorities in line. God first, and everything and everybody after that!

PRAYER:

Dear Lord,

Help me to make the adjustment of putting You first and everything else behind that. Even the opinions of others. Help me to be more concerned about pleasing You and making You smile.

In Jesus' name,
Amen

YOUR PRESENT DOESN'T FORECAST YOUR TOMORROW

One of the basic needs that humans have is to belong and to be loved. The need to be connected is so essential it is considered primal. Every living being wants connection.

It was so important to God for us to be interdependent that He even created animals to be part of a unit or community. A family of geese is a gaggle. A family of lions is a pride. A family of fish is a school. As for humanity, we have multiple names to describe our groupings – family, tribe, village, gang, troupe, sorority, fraternity, etc.

It is by these connections that individuals form their identity, and the group serves as a source of love. As a result of that belonging, people begin to form opinions and ideas about who they are in relationship to the group. These opinions and ideas then overflow into their interactions separate from the group. If the grouping is positive and nurturing, the individuals are able to develop into self-confident, strong, capable people. Conversely, if the group is dysfunctional, it can be damaging and devastating to its members.

The unfortunate thing is that many people are birthed into dysfunctional units. Because of the multiple damaging occurrences, individuals develop very low opinions of themselves. Those negative thoughts manifest into very destructive behaviors. This process supports the idea that is expressed by Proverbs 23:7 AMP, which says, *"As a man thinketh, so is he."* Our thoughts, which are generated by what is in our hearts, are manifested through our behaviors. If we have malice in our hearts, we begin to think evil thoughts and our behaviors are damaging to ourselves and to others. If we have jealousy in our hearts, then we think negative and hurtful thoughts and we behave in ways that demonstrate our jealousy, either by gossiping, being mean-spirited or belittling someone's existence.

In Genesis 29, we're introduced to Laban, who has two daughters: Leah, the oldest, and Rachel. Leah is referred to in less-than-favorable terms. In fact, the only thing that we know about Leah is that she is the oldest and that she is unattractive. However, when Rachel is introduced, we learn not only that she is the youngest and extremely attractive, but that she is favored and she is loved intensely by Jacob. In the words of the King James version of the Bible in verses 16 – 18a, *"And Laban had two daughters: the name of the elder was Leah, and the name of the younger was Rachel. Leah was tender eyed; but Rachel was beautiful and well favored. And Jacob loved Rachel..."*

Do you see what I see? The love and the appreciation of Rachel versus the disrespect given to Leah. Leah was held in such low regard that Laban, her father, tricked Jacob into taking Leah as one of his wives. Can you image how Leah must have felt when Laban shared his plan with her? How he must have told her that this is the way that he can ensure that she will be taken care of? How he framed it in the context of his love for her. The sad part is, Laban probably believed that what he was doing was an expression of love. He was securing her future.

In contrast, can you sympathize with Leah, knowing that her father thought that she would never find someone to love her fully for who she was? That nobody would recognize her specialness and want her to be their forever partner? Was she that unattractive, both in appearance and in character, that there wouldn't be anybody to love her?

As a result of her being considered damaged and *less than* as demonstrated by the actions of her father, she began to feel that she wasn't enough and wasn't deserving of true love and/or respect. Her low self-image then steered her behaviors.

Leah really believed that if she did enough, if she pleased Jacob enough, he would love her in totality. Therefore, she kept having children, and she even subjected her maidservant to having children with Jacob. All for the purpose of earning love. But Jacob's lack of love, respect or concern never changed. It remained the same; he was her husband not because he loved her but because he was tricked!

Even though Leah was unloved by Jacob, she was loved by God, and it was God who stepped in and put her in a place of honor. You see, in the Jewish culture, it is the oldest son of the family who receives the inheritance of the family, and the mother of that oldest son is held in high esteem by the community. So, when God saw the ill treatment of Leah, he allowed her to conceive and birth the oldest son. Look at God! He determines our worth, and He will make a way for His children to be the head and not the tail. Regardless of the value system of this world, God will work it all out to His children's good. Our *greater* is the result of His love!

Leah, the ugly and unloved, was placed in the forever seat of honor, being the mother of the firstborn and the guaranteed recipient of the family inheritance. Her greater was covered by His love and His love ensured that her greater would not, and could not, be ignored.

T3:

It doesn't matter what your right now looks like. It doesn't matter that, to the world, your life seems destined for discomfort and pain. God can, and He will, turn that around. He sees you, and He values you in totality. Praise be to God for all the great things He has done, is doing and will do!

PRAYER:

Dear God,

Thank you, God for seeing me and loving me completely. To You I will always be valuable, and I am grateful.

In the loving name of Jesus,
Amen

A Shift in Perspective

Change is necessary, but it is also difficult. So much so that there are studies, surveys and theories all committed to the necessity of change and how difficult it is for people to accept, to commit to and to actually make the change. Here's the kicker to it all: it doesn't matter your age, your experiences or your education – change is still HARD. Infants growing into toddlers and learning to walk – they fall, sometimes even injuring themselves, begging for their parents to pick them up, often reverting to crawling, all because it's too HARD! Teens becoming adults and attempting to find their place in the world – they teeter between remaining where they are and becoming what they need to be. Shoot, adults, moving from one job to the next, going from single to a committed relationship, going from college student to an employee embarking on an exciting new career, moving from their parents' house or a college dorm or from an apartment or leased dwelling to home ownership! It's all scary and it's H-A-R-D!

The same is true for everyone who chooses to be followers of Christ and accepts the gift of eternal life. The transition from living a life dictated by their own agenda to living a life that is submitted to the will of the Creator is HARD! The difficulty of the transition is demonstrated multiple times in the Bible:

- Psalms 119 shows the writer clinging to and loving God's word but having periods where he questions God's presence in his life and his continued dependence on God.
- Peter having to trust Jesus and move from the mindset of being a self-reliant business owner to being completely dependent on Jesus.
- Again, Peter having to move from the old paradigm of being governed by the Jewish law to being saved by grace and that all things created by God are good.
- Paul moving from being a persecutor of those who have accepted Jesus to being the most prolific writer of the New Testament and a fruitful planter of churches.
- The rich man that came to Jesus at night moving from being committed to his earthly riches to doing whatever is necessary to please God.
- Leah moving from the self-destructive mindset of being less than to embracing her value and worth and seeing herself as God saw her.

Why is change so difficult? FEAR! Pure and simple. To change, we have to shed what we think and believe to be true, divorce ourselves from all of our experiences and move to a place that is unknown. It forces us to expose and open ourselves up to the possibilities. Honestly, those possibilities can be both appealing and uncomfortable at the same time.

Once, I had an SUV that looked good, but when you would accelerate above a certain speed it would do a quick swerve and then straighten itself. Now, the first few times that occurred, it was frightening. So, I took it to the mechanic and determined that I just couldn't afford the repairs and I wasn't in a place where I could afford to purchase a new car. So, the most reasonable option was to purchase another used car. My father offered to help me purchase another used car and I told him that I wasn't sure that I wanted to do that. When he asked me why, I told him that I would rather deal with the devil that I already knew than to get a new devil from which I have no idea what to expect. You see, change is hard, and fear is real!

That fear is why people remain in very abusive and destructive relationships. They know the hell of their present, but they have learned how to operate and navigate within their hellish situation. To leave, to escape to a place that is unknown and foreign, requires that they begin to see themselves differently, and they will be forced to learn how to navigate the "new."

God knew that we tend to fear the unknown so intensely that all throughout the Bible, whenever He would present us with something new or whenever He was encouraging us to depend on Him, He would tell us not to fear. For examples, see Isaiah 41:10, Deuteronomy 31:6, 2 Timothy 1:7, Matthew 10:28 and I John 4:18. That's just five verses! Believe me, there are many, many more. Fear imprisons us and restrains us from changing the paradigm through which we view the world, ourselves and our situations.

When God sent Jesus to reclaim His lost children – to move us from where we were, Hell, and to move us to where He wants us to be, with Him in Heaven – He knew that the transition would be HARD and beset with fear! But even though it is hard to see ourselves as a new creation and to begin to operate as such, we must accept that the change is necessary and that our possibilities are greater than our present. In order for the Father to get us to the greater, we have to embrace the unknown and engage in the renewing process. That's called FAITH! In order for us to change and to transition to what God intends, we have to step out and step up and be willing to embrace the newness of our situation.

T3:

Change ain't easy, but it definitely is necessary! For the Father to get us to the greater, we have to embrace the unknown and engage in the renewing process. That's called FAITH!

PRAYER:

Dear God,

I want to trust You more than I fear the possibilities. Strengthen me as I submit to the process of change and as I begin the journey that will shift my paradigm and change my view of all things. My greater requires courage, and I believe that You will remain with me through it all.

In the mighty name of Jesus,
Amen

SELF-WORTH MATTERS

Psalm 8 speaks to a huge dilemma that plagues those of us who struggle with who we are, our self-view, versus who God has called and actually knows us to be. In the Psalm, David writes about the awesomeness of God and how He has done mighty works in the construction of the heavens and the earth, while at the same time He has created man and placed them in a place of high honor. What a mighty God we serve! What David is saying is that God can create and sustain such greatness that He really doesn't need us at all. However, God desires, loves and VALUES us, as written by David, at such a high level that He created us and placed us just beneath the angels. Placing us in a space of prestige and honor! Mind blowing!

For most of us, as we transition from sinner to sanctified, we struggle with thoughts of being unworthy. Unworthy of love, unworthy of blessings and unworthy of God's consideration. In fact, in Psalm 8:4 AMP, David asks, *"What is man that You are mindful of him...?"* Isn't that the question that we all ask? God, why do You consider me, why do You bless me, who am I to You?

Because we carry such burdens due to our past behaviors, negative experiences and poor self-image, we miss our value, our worth. Especially when we have felt that we were unloved by the actual folks that were supposed to express unconditional love and that are within our circles of daily interactions. It's difficult to embrace the love and value that an invisible God has for us when we experience the exact opposite from those we see every day. Couple that with the fact that we have to begin to believe and have faith that God, regardless of our deeds and circumstances, will never leave us nor will He forsake us, when so many have done just that. That just seems impossible.

However, it says in Isaiah 55 that God's thoughts are not our thoughts and His ways are not our ways. God recognizes that we cannot fathom His type of love because our deformed minds are not on His level. We can't fathom it because we don't have the mental prowess, capacity or capability.

This is where the paradigm shift is so necessary. We have to trust and have faith that God knows what He is doing and that His love is so deep, so wide and so vast that all we have to do is jump in and just swim.

Listen, God created us for greatness! In that same psalm, Psalm 8, David reaches the conclusion that God's awesomeness is above and beyond us. That He created all things in His perfection and then He placed us as stewards over it! Even in our imperfection, God sees such value in us that He trusts us with all that He has created. Why? Because He doesn't see us as man sees us. He sees us as He created us, in His image and likeness. So, if He is so awesome and valuable, there must be some awesomeness, value and worthiness in us too.

T3:

Step out of your self-image and step into your Godly worthiness! You've got value!

PRAYER:

Dear Father,

I want to see what You see. Open my eyes and shape my perspective.

In the name of Jesus,
Amen

Who Are You Trying to Satisfy

One of the Ten Commandments informs us that our God is a jealous God and that He doesn't want us to put anyone or anything before Him. His will and His desires should be primary in the life of the Believer.

That commandment has been taken all out of context by so many people, some of whom are well known and well respected. And because it has been taken out of context, the idea of being associated or connected to a person or personality that describes themselves as being jealous conjures up the image of something harmful and hurtful.

Beautifully, this jealousy, this holy and perfect jealousy, is extremely positive and should be embraced by every Believer. Our Creator is neither jealous of you nor would He harm you. Our Father's jealousy is based on His desire for you to see Him as your primary source for, well, everything. He wants to properly interact, bless and position you so that you can be extremely productive in kingdom building.

This is about us, Believers, putting God's desires before anything and everything else. He wants us to long to please and satisfy Him so that He can accomplish His desires through us. Here's the beauty in this: He doesn't have to use us, but He wants to! He uses us so He can have a full and enriched relationship with us! Having a complete picture of who He really is!

However, just like Leah, because of our fragile and distorted self-image, we spend most of our time trying to satisfy and impress people instead of desiring to impress our God. People, whose priority is to meet their own needs and who care very little about the well-being of others. That's who we tend to be concerned with. People who can't see what our God can and who, honestly, don't really care.

When I was in college (long enough ago that I'm keeping it vague), I so desperately wanted to be a part of an organization that I held in extremely high esteem. I believed that if I were a part of THAT organization, I would be better and be empowered to do bigger. I would surely be on the road to greater! I spent significant time, energy and brain power desiring and trying to get into their presence. I believed that if they got to know me, surely they would realize just how special I was. Going to great lengths to make sure that I wore the right clothes, with my hair and nails perfectly done, my face always flawless. I ensured that I was never in a space with people that were "less than remarkable" for fear that one of the members would see me and think that I was also less than remarkable. Oh my goodness, how my need for their approval consumed me. If at any time it seemed as if I fell out of their favor, I worked doubly hard to get it back. Lawd, looking back on it as I type these words, I am devastated and ashamed of my behavior. I needed their approval to validate my worth. That's so hard for me to admit.

Leah, because she couldn't see her worth or trust the love that God promised and continually articulated, worked, at her expense, to *MAKE* Jacob love and prefer her over her beautiful sister. Can't you relate to her struggle? Aren't there moments in your life that you can't see how amazing you are and so you work so hard to gain acceptance from people who could care less? Trying to meet their expectations so that they can approve your existence.

Unfortunately, because we lack self-love, we place the acceptance of others before the love of God. We forget, conveniently, that God is jealous and that He wants to be primary in our lives. I suspect that we do that because we put more faith in what we see (man) instead of what we can't (God). But what is faith if it is dependent on the visible – what can be seen? God requires our faith to be so intense and so strong that we rely on our spiritual connections more than on the physical. We then begin to function based on the trusting relationship that we've developed with and in God. Shifting our focus from satisfying man to satisfying someone who really cares for us and makes a lasting and impactful difference in our lives – God is where we must be concerned!

T3:

Seeking God's approval and satisfaction leads to a life filled with purposeful and prosperous living.

PRAYER:

God,

You are my priority, and my concerns are Your concerns. Your will is my will. Your desires are my desires. I will please You because I want to make You smile!

In the name of Jesus,
Amen.

You Can't Make Somebody Love You

In preparation for this writing, the song by the R&B artist Tank kept coming to mind: "I Can't Make You Love Me." The song chronicles the ending of a relationship and the need for the singer to have one last night with the partner before the inevitable breakup. It - is - so - sad. I researched the song and discovered that it was originally sung by the Country/Western singer Bonnie Raitt and then recorded by the pop artist Adele before Tank took a stab at it. That made me realize just how elementary the need to have someone truly love us is. It is such a driving and universal need that we spend an enormous amount of time and energy trying to get it. The need for love is not limited to any one type of person. It crosses all sectors of people and music genres – country, pop & R&B.

This desire for love pulls on us all in such a dramatic way that we place ourselves in (or we remain in) damaging and hurtful situations just so we can have and experience it! Look at Sis. Leah! Each time she or her maidservant would have a baby, she would declare that *this* baby should *make* Jacob love her.

In the scriptures, God closed Rachel's womb and opened Leah's because He saw that Leah was hated and He had compassion for her. However, with the birth of each child, the situation remained the same. Jacob's feelings for Sis Leah never changed, even though she was the mother of his first child and that child was a male child! He never held her in higher regard above Rachel. It was apparent that Rachel was the favored and deeply loved wife, but Leah continued to have more and more children, hoping to "win" Jacob's love. In fact, she had seven children and her maidservant had two, trying to gain Jacob's love. Yep, nine children and still not getting the love she desperately desired.

God's request is that we prioritize Him over anything and everything. He declares His love for us all throughout His word. His love for us is evident by the fact that every time we fall short, we miss the mark and we disobey His word, He provides us with an escape from the consequences of our sinful behaviors. When we were bound by the law, God provided His children with rituals and opportunities to escape the ultimate consequence for our disobedience, which was eternal damnation. Then He provided us with Jesus and allowed grace to cover His children. Giving us the gift of repentance that would keep us in good standing with our Father. He provided us with Jesus to atone for our sins, opening the door to a Heavenly eternal existence and repairing the damaged and severed relationship. That's love! We did nothing to deserve it or to have the privilege to experience it. It just is! This love is all about our God. It just is because God is who He is – LOVE!

HERE'S the beauty of Leah's seemingly painful and depressing story. After the birth of her last child, a daughter, instead of

59

focusing on the desired love of Jacob, she began to focus on God, the one that had always loved her and had never left her. Hey now, the paradigm shift has occurred! Instead of expecting Jacob to come and profess his undying love for her, she announced that she will instead praise God! Her attention shifted and was realigned. Instead of looking at man to be the source of the love she desired, she began to focus on God, the very essence of love. She stopped putting man over God. That's realignment! The perfect response to her finally getting her priorities in order is that she gave God praise! The praise that He desires and the praise that He deserves!

T3:

True love doesn't require you to do anything to receive it, because the one true love is the love of our God! Just put God first, watch how He shows up and then give Him His praise!

PRAYER:

Dear God,

Thank you for being just who You are – love. Your love is not contingent on anything that I do, but it has everything to do with who You are. I freely experience Your love. Remind me to praise You for Your unconditional love. Remind me that You are the source of my being. Praise You, my God. I appreciate You for who You are – LOVE!

In the lovely name of Jesus,
Amen

REDIRECT:

Direct (someone or something) to a new or different place or purpose

Rahab: Joshua 2

A woman who lived in Jericho that was in the Promised Land of Canaan. She assisted the Israelites in capturing the city by hiding the two spies that were scouting out opposition. As a result of her assistance, she was able to save herself and her family.

YOU'RE VALUABLE

When starting my career, I took my first job with a long-standing girls' organization whose mission is to help in developing girls of courage, confidence and good character who make the world a better place. Now, I had limited exposure to this organization. Honestly, I hadn't participated in the program when I was younger, and I didn't have knowledge of any of my family members ever participating. To be real, it was common knowledge that this organization did not have a strong presence in communities where families had limited resources and/or were people of color. The only real encounter that I had with the organization was buying from their yearly fundraiser.

After graduating from college and after making some drastic changes in my professional course, I needed a job. That's when I came across the posting for a vacancy with the organization. Admittedly, I was hesitant to apply even though I had many, if not all, of the listed qualifications. What I didn't have was a deep knowledge of or respect for the organization. However, I submitted my application packet and just prayed that I would get an interview. Within days, I received a call to schedule the interview and I began to prep. What I discovered was that all

YOU'RE VALUABLE

the current staff had extensive organizational knowledge and experience. In fact, 100% of them had been members as young girls. I began to question, due to my lack of knowledge, my not being a member as a child and because I didn't fit the demographics of their present staff or membership, whether I should even show up for the interview. I really considered calling and cancelling, thinking that I should wait until I found something that I was a better "fit" for. Maybe I could find a job where they could value my total personhood and thus respect my viewpoint and see my potential contribution. But I interviewed anyway, preparing myself for getting a "Thanks, but no thanks" result.

On many occasions I've talked myself out of opportunities. Many of those opportunities, when I look back, could have positioned me for greater. If I had not listened to the negative tapes that continually played in my head, I would have made greater strides professionally and, I believe, personally. If only I had just seized the moment, relied on God and seen my own value. Many times in my life I have been my own worst enemy. I haven't needed anyone else to get in my way. I did that all by myself. By getting in my own way and by allowing fear to be bigger than my faith, I've sat by the wayside and watched others as they moved forward with fruitful careers or made strategic connections that would catapult them into their greater. All the while, I sat and berated myself for not stepping out, valuing what I could have added and then just doing it!

In Joshua 2, we are introduced to Rahab, the harlot. If you are unfamiliar with the term, a harlot is the same as a prostitute; a woman of the evening; a call girl. However, Rahab wasn't just a prostitute; she was the owner of the business. To say that it was

66

a *reprehensible* occupation is an understatement. I'm sure that Rahab didn't go to work thinking that her work was honorable or that it was a positive contribution to the community in any way. I'm sure the only thing that she found to be valuable about her employment was the financial resources that it provided for her family.

Here's what I love about Rahab! Even though she was a harlot and wasn't held in very high regard, especially by the women of her community, I'm sure, she did understand that in this particular situation, the hiding and directing of the Israelite spies, she had added value. She realized that despite how others felt about her and even how she may have felt about herself, she was going to use her value to be helpful to the spies while simultaneously helping her family. She didn't waste time trying to talk herself out of it, she just stepped out and did it! Because she did, she was able to save herself, save her family and guarantee a place with the Father in eternity.

Your greater can't wait for you to change the minds of others or of yourself! You are valuable to the Father, and you must use your value for all it is worth so that God can be glorified.

Oh, by the way, I got the job. Not only did I get it, but I excelled and was able to leverage that experience into greater professional opportunities. Yep, I used the value that was God-given and was allowed to optimize my potential!

T3:

To progress into our greater, we must develop an "in spite of" Spirit. In spite of the opinion of man, I will rely on the opinion of God as the measurement of my worth.

PRAYER:

Dear Lord,

It is by Your opinion that I will determine my value, and I thank You for loving me so much that You find value in me when I can't see it for myself. Keep me focused on You and maintaining a desire to please You.

In Jesus' name I pray,
Amen

RISK IS REQUIRED

I have a friend that does not hesitate to take risks. She will try almost anything! Skydiving – she's done it! Jumping from a cliff into a body of water –check! Traveling out of the country alone –completed! Left a job before having a replacement –yep! Moving to a strange land –done! Seemingly, she has no fear. She is willing to take the risk and do the unthinkable (at least what is unthinkable to me). When I asked her why she risks both life and limb, doing what I consider crazy, her response was simple: "Why not?" I asked her to go deeper, and she explained that she never thinks about the potential loss. She always focuses on what she can gain. She believes that she has enriched her life in such a way that everything she has engaged in has been worth the potential risk.

Honestly, I can't get with that type of thinking. For me, it's always about what could be lost and who would my actions negatively impact. Will my family be hurt by my risky behaviors? Would my finances be negatively impacted? And what about my reputation?

As a result of my aversion to risk, I've missed out on so much. As I've gotten older, I think back on the multiple opportunities

I've let go by because I didn't want to take the risk. How many fond memories and wonderful experiences I would have had if only I had taken the risk!

Risk, exposure to real or perceived danger, is the partner to fear. The whole reason we say some things are risky is because we fear what *might* occur. Let me be clear: some things are risky and should be feared! Jumping in front of a bullet or experimenting with addictive drugs – that's risky and I want you to stay away from those types of behaviors. However, there are opportunities we avoid and dismiss only because we are fearful. We fear what might happen and how it may be uncomfortable, never considering what positive thing may occur because we took the chance.

In I Corinthians 2, Paul boldly states that he is afraid to preach in front of the Corinthians. Why? Because Paul understood that the message he was going to share was not what the Corinthians wanted to hear. It didn't line up with what they understood or valued. Paul knew that his message could lead to him suffering bodily harm or being ostracized or jailed!

However, Paul leaned into the fear, took the risk and preached the message of Jesus, His saving power and the need to be converted. Why did he move forward even though he was fearful? He proceeded because he hoped others would be converted! That was his calling: God being glorified and the Kingdom being edified. Simple!

That was Rahab! She understood the risk of hiding the spies, helping them to scout the land and then giving them directions for safe passage home. Although being found out was a huge risk to her, her family and her business, she leaned into her fear and she did it!

Not only did she hide the spies, she was audacious enough to ask them to spare her life and the lives of her family! Now, that's not only risky; it's nervy. She dared to do the unthinkable. She was willing to give up everything she knew and understood to be true, hoping that she would gain greater. Who does that?

Actually, that is what God wants us all to do. We must take the risk, give up everything we know and understand and trust Him to be Lord and Captain of our lives.

We are familiar with the life of the unsaved or the life of the right now. It's a safe and comfortable place for us. But it is not where or what God wants for us. We must take the risk, accept Jesus and begin to learn what being a disciple really means; only then will we begin to have the benefit of the multiple blessings that are afforded us. For us to reap the greater, we must assume the risk and just jump right in.

Because Rahab moved beyond her fear and envisioned and embraced the possibilities, she was able to save herself and her entire family. She gained life in eternal victory, the greater, because she took the risk. Just think, if we would lean into the calling that God has for every believer and take the risk and jump, greater is the only result!

T3:

Greater is much bigger and better than remaining where we are because we are fearful and comfortable. For us to reap the greater, we must assume the risk and just jump right in.

PRAYER:

Dear Lord,

I desire greater, doing the work that You have for me. I desire the courage to just jump. Remind me that You are always with me. Then just hold my hand as I take the risk, lean in and just do it.

In the precious name of Jesus,
Amen

KNOW IT WHEN YOU HEAR IT

As humans, we are naturally skeptical and hesitant to believe others. We do not often participate in certain activities because of the knowledge we believe we lack. This is especially true if we've never seen or heard of it being done before. It's not part of our history. For example, this new trend to invest and use cryptocurrency. Cryptocurrency is everywhere. I've heard about it on the news, read about it and had friends explain it. Even some of my favorite actors and athletes are endorsing it. All I've heard about crypto is how it is the currency of the future and that we need to get on board. If we're not going to start using it, at least we should invest in it.

Now, I've researched cryptocurrency and I've spoken with my husband and I ain't buying it! It is just *too* foreign to me. All my life, the only type of currency I've been exposed to is either the dollar bill or the credit card. Oh, and I've used checks, understanding that they are backed by the dollar. Honey, this crypto stuff. I do not understand it, and I just can't! I just can't see the benefit. The risk is just too much and I'm not willing to jump into it. I'm sure when Apple, Microsoft and other tech companies hit the scene, they faced the same skepticism. People would not invest because it was too foreign to what people knew to be true.

In Joshua 2, Rahab talked with the spies and proclaimed the fact that she and her community had heard the stories about the greatness of their God. She told the stories that she'd heard about what their God had done for the Israelites, the chosen ones, just because He, God, was so awesome. How God had freed them from bondage, led them across the Red Sea and destroyed their enemy. How God had allowed His people to utterly destroy the mighty armies of the Amorites and others. It was because of these stories of victories made possible by their God, and her community's belief that their God would continue to bless them so that they could claim the land He had promised, that the Canaanites were fearful of them.

Most importantly, Rahab believed the stories and testimonies of God and the victories that He had given to His chosen people. Even though it was stories about a God that she had never encountered, personally. This God was not a part of anything she knew or understood. The only thing she had to rely on was the testimonies about the God of the Chosen. What she also knew was that she was not one of the Chosen!

So, what made Rahab first believe and then ask if she and her family could be benefactors of the greatness and goodness of their God? It is because she, first, *heard* the testimonies of the greatness and goodness of their God. In Romans 10:14, Paul asks how people can be saved unless they hear. It emphasizes the importance of the sharing of God & His greatness through the testimonies of His people. Now, specifically, he is talking about the importance of the preacher, and also speaking about how important it is for everybody to tell the story. It is by the testimonies of God's people that others are exposed to the awesome possibilities available because of the connection that Believers have with the Father.

Not only did she hear the testimonies, but she believed them to be true. She exemplifies trusting not in what she could see but in the unseen God that they testified about. She heard it, trusted it and she took the opportunity to get it! To get to her greater! She didn't allow her opportunity to pass her by. She knew in her heart that this was her chance, and she took it.

T3:

You've heard how when Believers follow God, trust His promises and just do it, that their future is greater than their present. Know it when you hear it and then do it!

PRAYER:

My God,

Open my ears to hear the testimonies of Your people so that I can be encouraged to take the chance and experience greater!

In the powerful name of Jesus,
Amen

SEIZE THE MOMENT

It is so funny to me the curious and even judgmental looks that I get when I tell people I see myself in Rahab in many ways, and how I wish I were more like her in others. I realize that most people want to see themselves as a more upstanding and respectable Biblical woman. Most people want to see themselves as the Virtuous Woman, Deborah the Judge, Queen Esther, Ruth, the mother of the kinsmen redeemer, or Mary, the mother of Jesus. Shoot, many would rather be the bent-over woman or the woman with the issue of blood than to be Rahab the harlot. At least those women were in the right place at the right time – encountering Jesus and being healed and made whole. But Rahab – what qualities would anyone find appealing?

Believe me, I get it, but for me and my experiences, Rahab is the closest to where I was before I met and developed a true and authentic relationship with my Lord and Savior. Not that I was a harlot, by any means. Never did I ever consider that as a viable way to support either myself or my family. However, I did have questionable behaviors that could be considered damaging to all that I was trying to accomplish and to the lifestyle I was attempting to create. Also, as I continue my journey of transformation, I realize that we all, pre–Jesus, have had, and still *have,* some questionable behaviors that we need to be redeemed from and repentant of. If we didn't, there wouldn't be or have been a need for Jesus to come and atone for our sins. Mostly, I have come to understand that I ain't where I should be. As I proclaim to be a child of the King, I've got a lot of work to do to get better. But I share that same situation with all of you! We all were saved from something so we could freely and confidently move to our greater. What we must equally embrace is that we all have a long way to go.

Now, there is still an area in which I wish I was MORE like Rahab. Close your mouth and don't be shocked. She was a risk taker and, when she saw an opportunity that could change the trajectory of her life, she seized the moment. Ms. Rahab did not let fear paralyze her. As we discussed previously, she embraced the testimonies of the awesomeness of our God and when she saw a chance to be saved, to get in on the action, to be connected to and acquainted with God and His chosen people, she jumped at it! She did not let fear of being a harlot, being Gentile and not one of the chosen, or the possibility that the spies would reject her offer keep her from what she believed was beneficial for both her and her family. She saw the door, opened it and she walked right through it.

There are so many opportunities presented to us that we allow to just go by without taking advantage. We (myself included) begin to enumerate all of the reasons why we should not jump into the deep waters of opportunities. We run the tapes in our heads that tell us:

- I am not prepared,
- I don't know enough to do that,
- My past is a little too sketchy and/or shady,
- What if they find out about this and that, and
- I don't have the best or the right lineage.

I could go on and on. We suffer from inactivity due to fear. We hesitate to take risks because we are immature and we don't embrace the power that God has given to each of us. We don't trust that God won't ever leave or forsake us. We won't stop, evaluate the opportunity, look for God in it, rely on His grace and then do it! We fear failure and defeat. We hide behind the excuse that whatever this thing is may not be God ordained.

Here's what I've experienced and come to understand: I need to lean into trusting that God is in this thing with me, and if I happen to fail, He will lift me, dust me off, help me to find the lesson and then equip me for the next time! The "failure" is to strengthen and prepare me. My next will be greater than my now, so I must be fully prepared to handle the greater.

Beloved, it is God's desire that we prosper. That whatever we are engaged in, if it is for His name's sake, it will be successful. Therefore, if you evaluate the opportunity and determine that God will get the glory then, take the darn risk!

T3:

Your greater is on the other side of the risk! Seize it.

PRAYER:

Dear Lord,

If You are in it, let me see it so that I may seize it. It is by Your strength that I will elevate to greater. Therefore, I will trust that this opportunity is saturated by Your desire for me to move to the next, the greater.

In Jesus' name,
Amen

YOU'RE COVERED

Maslow's Pyramid of the Hierarchy of Needs describes the five stages of human growth. Each stage, as believed by Maslow, must be satisfied before someone can become a fully actualized person. Once an individual progresses past the initial need to breathe, to be fed and to have shelter, the next need that must be satisfied is the need to feel safe – personally, financially, and with regard to health. Until we can feel as if we have a safe place to live, can receive a decent meal and that we can maintain a reasonable portion of health and strength, it's difficult for us to contemplate or consider better or greater. Our minds are occupied with just making it to the next – the next place to sleep, the next meal, the next safe place!

In Psalm 55:22, Believers are encouraged to give God our cares and concerns, and He will sustain us because He will not allow His children, those made righteous through His son Jesus, to be moved. God provides us with the necessary covering and the assurance that He is our protection.

This is demonstrated in Joshua 2 when the spies inform Rahab that if she and her family remain in the house, they will be covered and protected – they would live. Really, what God did was reward Rahab for her trust and faithfulness and for taking the risk. In her stepping out on her faith and believing the testimonies of God, she, along with her family, will gain access to living abundantly both on earth and eternally in Heaven with God. She is eternally covered!

Throughout the Bible, Believers are reminded of the intentions of God. Reminded that He loves us and that he wants us to experience victories in Him. Victories that we wouldn't have the privilege of winning outside of Him. Here, God expresses that He is a fulfiller of promises and that He is faithful.

What's interesting in the conversation between the spies and Rahab is that the spies warn Rahab that the promise of protection is not extended to anyone *outside* of the house. The people that are relying on their own power will not be spared.

We, as Believers, are eternally covered; however, we must maintain our focus on God and His desires and not our own. We cannot rely on our own power to guide, protect or to propel us to our greater. If we do that, we lose concentration, become impatient with the process and begin to believe that we can do it alone. When we step outside of God's covering, we open ourselves up to the consequences of being uncovered. Not uncovered to the point of losing our status of eternal life. Rather, we'd lose the covering and protection from suffering the consequences of our poor decisions.

This is not mentioned to frighten you to a point of immobility. This is a warning to encourage you to trust God and to keep Him primary as we move forward to our greater. Really, our greater shouldn't be so much of our focus that it becomes more important and bigger than the one that is making it all possible! Yes, God covers and protects us, and He wants us to launch into our greatness. But He desires for us to keep our priorities in order so that He can continue to support our evolving to our greater.

T3:

You're covered! Now, prioritize, evaluate, and do!

PRAYER:

Dear Father,

Thank you for Your covering. As long as I remain in You, I will be victorious. My victories are because of You, and I am extremely thankful.

Praising You in Jesus' name,
Amen

TRUST GOD

I'm sure you've heard the saying "Fool me once, shame on you. Fool me twice, shame on me." Also, the one that has been attributed to the great Maya Angelou: "When somebody SHOWS you who they are, BELIEVE them!" (emphasis mine). Well, unfortunately, because some of the harsh lessons I've experienced, these sayings have become an integral part of how I relate to and interact with people. Whenever I let people in, I've been hurt. Thus, I have difficulty allowing people to get close. I can't give you the exact moment when it changed for me, when the walls started to go up. I think it is the compounding of a series of life events.

When I was in elementary school, I would take all kinds of risks, engaging in multiple experiences and developing relationships with all types of people. Honestly, I often enjoyed myself. However, the older I got, more often than I care to count, people would repeatedly betray my trust, hurt my feelings and set me up for the letdown. Because of continual disappointments and the wounds that I just couldn't recover from, I became hesitant to engage and interact with others. In fact, I was frightened of and hesitant to take risks that would require me to trust and depend on others.

That's why I am horrible at the very important professional skill of networking. Why would I put myself out there just so I can be betrayed once again? The pain just grew to be too much. So, I remained, and I often still remain, in my space of mistrust.

Here's what's so sad about my inability to trust: I have missed out on being more useful in kingdom building. Although I have desired to have God use me in continuing the work of kingdom building on a grander scale, it hasn't happened because I've tied God's hands. By not trusting others and ultimately not trusting Him, I have limited my effectiveness in the will that God has for my life (how's that for transparency?).

Yep, I said it. See, I am a strong believer that God wants to bless. Shoot, I believe that God wants to bless so much that He stands waiting, searching and looking for every opportunity possible to bless His children. My problem was that my belief stopped at you. Yes, I believed that God wanted to bless, but because of all of the hurt, pain and difficulties that I'd encountered, I didn't believe or trust that God wanted to bless me. Why would He? I came with too much baggage. I'd been through too much. I'd been hurt too many times and hadn't been able to recover. I was too flawed to be blessed.

Because of my lack of trusting anyone, including God, I wasn't standing in my calling. Consequently, I wasn't being fruitful in kingdom building. I was just going through the motions, faking it.

Then, one day while having a full-blown pity party with tears, runny nose and tissues, knowing that I wasn't doing what God had called me to do, I opened my Bible to Psalm 91. I was looking for some relief from my pain. Right there in verses 1 &

2 I read, "*Those who live in the shelter of the Most High* will find rest in the shadow of the Almighty. *This I declare about the Lord: He alone is my refuge, my place of safety; He is my God,* and I trust Him" (emphasis mine). Bam! Mic drop! My mind was blown. Since I live under the covering of my God, I will experience rest. What kind of rest? For me, rest from worrying about being betrayed and hurt or being a failure and unsuccessful. Rest from being concerned about what could happen or even about what has happened. My God has given me rest.

Actually, He reminded me, in that very moment, that He can handle anything that may come my way, but I have to trust and allow Him to handle it. I've got to do His work and open myself up to people, not worrying about the who, what, when, where and hows. I'm just expected to lean into Him and let Him do what He does best. Even though I've suffered some devastating blows and losses, I have to believe and trust that God has it (and had it) under control. Why? Because I live in His shelter and there, I am safe, sheltered from all hurt, harm and danger.

Yes! We, as Believers, will suffer some blows and setbacks and endure some difficulties. Yes, it will sometimes seem as if God has left us. But that's when our trust and faith must kick in. It is at those times, when we feel as if we can't do it anymore, that we sit in His shelter, rest and watch Him go to work. It is all working together for our good, so we must just trust and rest. Yep, those are the key words: trust and rest, rest and trust.

T3:

God is our resting place, so we can't concern ourselves with the potential of disappointment or pain. That could happen, but God's got you! Just rest in His awesomeness and watch Him do His work. Trusting that it is all for our good.

PRAYER:

Dear Lord,

I believe that whatever I encounter, whatever occurs in my life, regardless how disappointing or painful, You've got me. You are my shelter, my protector and my provider. I just have to rest in You. Thank you!

In the restful name of Jesus,
Amen

THE UNEXPECTED

Have you ever experienced something so unexpected that it took you a moment to recover? Be it a good experience or not, it still took you a moment to really realize what just happened. I have those experiences sometimes, and I am always baffled by how I never get used to the feeling. Yes, my husband and I can go out to dinner and the waiter will inform us that our meal has been taken care of! What!? Or when I go to the cash register to purchase something and the sale was 75% off rather than 50%! What!? I'll take that. Or I received a pay increase and it wasn't the normal time of year. Or, on the flip side, I go out to start the car and it doesn't start. Or, during a rainstorm the sump pump in the house decides not to work!

One of the biggest times where I was unexpectedly surprised was at the birth of my daughter. After two or three days of labor (it was all a blur), I thought that I was going to be so angry when she finally arrived. But when she got here and I looked at her, funny shaped head and all, all of the anger and even some of the pain suddenly disappeared. The unexpected!

The unexpected happens most often during my times of Bible study. Preparing for a lesson or just in my quiet time of review, bam, I get a revelation, or I read something that I've read numerous times before and will gain a different perspective. A new insight. The unexpected!

One night, I was reading the genealogies of Jesus recorded in both Matthew and Luke. Yes, the versions are different; there are reasons for that, but it would require me to transition this book from a devotional to a study (my writing coach already said that this is actually that). However, when studying Matthew's version, I noticed something different. Buried in the *begets* and the *fathers to this and that person*, there in verse 5 is the unexpected: "*Salmon begot Boaz by Rahab…*" (Matthew 1:5).

Yep, just in case you missed it, Rahab the harlot, the great, great grandmother to King David, is in the genealogy of Jesus. Bam! The unexpected!

How does that happen? How does the unexpected become the reality? Well, in this case, Rahab was bodacious enough to jump out on faith and rely on the testimonies of those who were considered the chosen people. She took the risk and got into the house so that she was covered. She saw the opportunity to get into alignment with God to discover what her possibilities and future could be if she developed a relationship with the true and living God. She seized the moment! Because of her strong desire to get into the house, to find rest, she was able to not only change the lives of her and her family, but she was used by God to orchestrate salvation for you and me! (Are you running? If you ain't, you just should be!)

Now do you see why I so identify with Rahab? Yes, she started out as a harlot, someone with a sketchy and questionable existence.

But with one decision, in one moment, the moment she decided to get within the will of the Creator, she altered her outcome for eternity. She is the ultimate example of not allowing her present to imprison the possibilities of her future. She redirected her possible end. An end slated for eternal damnation. She redirected it to a life eternal. A life that would eternally be spent with our Creator in forever rest. And she remains in a space of prestige in the lineage of Jesus!

Our present is not permanent, and our future is full of positive possibilities. As long as we hang on to the hand of our Creator and follow His direction and not our own, our lives can experience a redirection that can only be orchestrated by the power of our God!

T3:

> Don't be paralyzed by what you know. Trust in the One who designs and designates your future.

PRAYER:

> Dear God,
>
> Redirect my life. Open my mind to the possibilities so that I can boldly take advantage of the opportunities to move into my greatness. It is because of You that redirection is possible. I will look for the unexpected! Surprise me, Lord!
>
> In the name of Jesus,
> Amen.

REDEFINE:

To define or describe differently

Hannah: I Samuel 1 – 2:11

One of the two wives of Elkanah. She suffered the chastisement and teasing of the other wife, Peninnah, because she could not have children. Eventually, she gave birth to Samuel, whom she gave to God for His service.

Your Circumstances Don't Define You

Have you ever noticed that people become associated with and connected to their circumstances? That's how they are described. It usually goes like, "You know her, she's the one who has been sick for a while." Or "You know him, he's the one who has all those baby mommas." Or "She's the one who just got that new job and had to quit because she couldn't find decent childcare." I could go on and on. I've even done it myself. My husband will tell me a story, or he is recounting his day and he'll have to remind me who Sister or Brother so-and-so is. Often, I will respond, for the purpose of clarity, with a certain circumstance or situation that I associate with that person. Have you ever noticed that it also occurs in the Bible? It often happens with women – the woman with the issue of blood, the bent over woman, the woman at the well. No names, just circumstances.

Although others tend to describe us by our situations or circumstances, what's sad is that we do it to ourselves – high school dropout, single mother with three children under the age of five, too old, too young, ill prepared, too this, too that, too the other. What makes it doubly sad is that we allow those portrayals to become the way we navigate life, interact with others and make decisions. We'll deny ourselves an opportunity because we failed at it before, or we won't participate in something because others may be in attendance and we fear their judgments and opinions. We base our next on what has happened or what is occurring. Never do we stop, look for God and then move forward.

Hannah fell victim to becoming her circumstance. She was married to a wonderful man, Elkanah, who loved her immensely, but she couldn't have children. In fact, Elkanah would go to great lengths to demonstrate his love, giving to her more of whatever he possessed. In fact, he gave more to her than to his other wife who was the mother of his children. Hannah was so focused on her circumstance that she couldn't see the love that surrounded her.

Now, admittedly, during Biblical times, the bearing of children, especially male children, was both important and prestigious. A woman was considered "less than" if she was unable to first, have children, and secondly, have a male child. Since that was the cultural norm, Hannah was burdened with the thought that she was a disgrace to herself, to her husband and to the community. She was so fixated on what she didn't have that she became depressed and wouldn't eat. Due to her depression, she missed everything that God was providing. She missed it because her vision was clouded by what she did not have rather than being focused on what she did.

Beloved, change your perspective by changing what you focus on. If you are allowing your circumstances to dictate and determine who you are, start looking up and not around. Your present circumstances are not the determinant of your greater!

Your circumstances, your challenges, your difficulties are the playing field where God will operate and move on your behalf. Your right now is not what defines you and it surely shouldn't be the thing that stops you. It is in these places, the places where it seems impossible to man, that God does His greatest work. It is also in these spaces that you get stronger; your faith increases. In the midst of the impossible is where people get to witness the awesomeness of God and where He gets the glory!

Jesus states in Luke 18:27 that what is impossible to man is possible with God. It is in those impossible, dark and dismal circumstances that we must watch, pray and remain in God's hands. It is from that vantage point, that front row seating, that we get to watch God do what only He can.

T3:

In the midst of the impossible is where people get to witness the awesomeness of God and where He gets the glory! You may not be able to see the movement of God, but you can trust that He is in your midst and operating on your behalf.

PRAYER:

Dear Lord,

Keep me focused on the promise and not the problem. Remove my disbelief and replace it with trust. I will watch and pray as You complete Your wonderous works in my life.

In the miraculous name of Jesus,
Amen.

TORMENTORS AND OPPOSITION ARE REAL

Haters, opposition, tormentors, antagonists, adversaries, foes – all the words! They all mean the same thing: someone who attempts to stand in the path of your getting to greater. Or, they are people who are angry because you're making progress toward your greater. Since the beginning of man and the introduction of sin, jealousy and envy – or just pure evil – have been present. The challenge is that we do not allow them to become distractors to our stepping into our calling and getting to our greater.

Hannah had a constant tormentor in the person of Peninnah, the other wife of Elkanah. Peninnah, the mother of Elkanah's children, was not satisfied with her prestigious position in the family and she felt the need to torment Hannah, continually. Was she jealous of the love that Elkanah continually expressed toward Hannah? Was she envious of Hannah's light? The source for her desire to continuously antagonize Hannah is never revealed. What we know is that Hannah's hater was forever present and added to the apparent pain that she was already experiencing. Haters are going to hate!

When my husband became a pastor and we relocated, I naively believed that we were going to move, start the work, link with others in the ministry and glorify God in the process of adding to the kingdom. So, if there was something to attend, we did. If there was a group looking for partnerships, if it was within the will of God, we partnered. We got involved on the local, state and national levels, both politically and in the ministry. We developed relationships that we believed were fruitful and supportive. We found our lane and we got in it. Life was good. That was, until it wasn't. Suddenly, and without any warning, things began to change. As we began to move the ministry forward, waves of opposition began to confront us. One punch here from someone we would have never suspected and another blow from a different direction.

My husband never seemed to be phased by the fiery darts launched our way. But for me, it was a different story. Because of my previously admitted trust issues, I was devastated by every blow. I would turn over and over in my mind the slights, the mean words, the undercover resentment, the incorrect information being shared in the community, the accusations, the falsehoods. These actions were often being either generated from or supported and encouraged by persons in the Christian community, those who were supposed to be about God's business. I cannot describe the pain I felt, nor how, with each disappointment, I became less and less effective in the ministry.

I was so focused on the things around me that I took my eyes off Jesus. Just like Peter. When he stepped out of the boat, focused on Jesus, he walked on water. But when his focus changed, he began to drown. I too began to drown. Ministry wasn't fun anymore. It wasn't enjoyable. It wasn't fulfilling. With everything we did, I was more concerned about what people thought, what they would say, what they would do and how it would read in the community. It was depressing and extremely exhausting.

I forgot about all of the Biblical verses that inform us that trials and tribulations are to be expected. I forgot about how many from the religious community launched rocks of criticism, doubt and lies towards Jesus and His disciples. Those launching the rocks of discourse hoped that something would derail the ministry's progress. I forgot about Paul and the multiple times he was jailed, beaten and thrown outside of cities all because he was engaged in the ministry.

I forgot because I kept looking around instead of looking up!

Our job as Believers is not to avoid difficulties, tormentors or distractors. That's impossible. What is possible is that we can remain single-minded and focused on our shared purpose – to embrace our calling, engage in ministry and glorify the Father. That's all. That's it.

T3:

Haters will hate, but they don't have to distract! We cannot allow them to become distractors to our stepping into our calling and getting to our greater. Let God handle them; we must remain focused on Him.

PRAYER:

Father God,

Thank you for having plans for me that transcend my haters. I will believe that Your intentions for my life will come to pass.

In the intentional name of Jesus,
Amen

ACCEPT LOVE

I am amazed by how people always seem to maintain focus on the negative aspects of life. We focus so intensely on the negative that we miss the beautifully positive that is right in front of us. We concentrate on who didn't come rather than those who did. We count the number of people who didn't clap rather than those who gave the standing ovation. We remember the mean and hurtful things that people have said rather than the uplifting and positive. We chronicle those times we've been mistreated rather than the times we've received countless expressions of love and appreciation. It's as if our vision suffers from selective glaucoma, unable to see those things that will add positively to our lives. On the other hand, we have 20/20 crystal clear vision for those things that subtract from our self-esteem and cause us to think and feel differently about ourselves. It's as if we want to be hurt, having hearts that are filled with pain and memories that demean and damage our self-perceptions. We look for evidence to affirm the negative and we disregard the relationships and the opportunities to be uplifted, to build and to encourage ourselves.

When reading I Samuel 1:5 – 8, I realized that this behavior ain't new (my mother is reading this wondering why she paid all that money for my college education). Mostly, when we have hurtful experiences and we begin to have those all-too-familiar damaging and debilitating thoughts of not being enough, we believe that we are the only ones who feel this way or have to endure such difficulties. Immediately and often without notice, we begin to engage in damaging and self-defeating behaviors. Our minds spiral into thinking we are alone. We're alone in feeling unloved. We're alone in feeling that everyone or most people are against us. We're alone in believing that God wants us to suffer and that He has left us to endure the difficulties of life without any support or covering. Here, in these verses, we see Hannah concentrating on the negative – missing the love and encouragement that is available, waiting for her acceptance and engagement. Here, her husband is desperately trying to fill the hole that is left by the fact that she is unable to conceive and have children. He continually expresses and demonstrates his love and care for her by giving her more, but she either misses, ignores or discounts his efforts.

As evidenced here, the feelings and behaviors of missing the positive and accentuating the negative are not new. We have all missed opportunities to be and to feel love. God, like Elkanah, is always demonstrating His love for us. Always blessing, always providing, always protecting, always opening doors, always closing doors that will cause harm, always covering, always lifting and always loving. We just miss it, ignore it and overlook it. Because we miss it, we have to endure unnecessary pain and misery.

Here's the worst part of missing love, its expressions and the opportunities to embrace it: we retard and stagnate our ability to dramatically improve our effectiveness in operating in our calling and getting to our greater. Focusing on the negative and participating in self-defeating behaviors take time and energy away from progressing our calling forward. God wants to use us fully for His purpose. We can't get to the *fully* when we are focused on the incomplete.

T3:

God is love, and He deeply loves us. God is the Master Builder who can and will fill any hole in our hearts. It is our job to seek Him and then allow Him to do His work. We've got to seek and accept His love.

PRAYER:

Father God,

You are the essence of love, and I choose to accept it.

In the loving name of Jesus,
Amen

Prayer is Powerful

My husband and I have been together for about 27 years – six months of dating, one and a half years of engagement and about 25 years of marriage. OOH WHEE! When I put it out there like that, I realize we've been in this thing for a minute! What I learned very early on is that if I wanted something from Evans, I needed to make my request known. I couldn't just expect him to figure it out. See, I tried that "he should know what I want" approach. Let's just say that his response to my need was less than stellar. Now, that wasn't his fault, although I tried to make him feel as if he should have known better. But, again, it wasn't his fault. I needed to make my needs known. In order to do that, I needed to open my mouth! Once that lesson was learned and I started to just be blunt, bold and intentional about my needs, wants and desires, our lives became so much easier and our marriage was that much happier.

That same strategy of verbalizing my needs not only works for my husband, it also works with God. We all should know that our earthly relationships and interactions are just dress rehearsals for how God wants us to be relational and interactive with Him. God uses our earthly lives to inform us of our spiritual expectations.

God expects us to have such an intimate and close relationship that we are fearless in our communications with Him. Meaning, we know that God wants to hear from us, and we know that He wants to respond to our needs. Shoot, we know that He already knows our wants and our needs. However, He also desires for us to be conversational with Him. He wants us to tell Him what we want and then be expectant of receiving it.

By opening our mouths, often referred to in the Bible as crying out, we signify to God that we trust Him with the request, that we expect a response and that we trust that He will deliver, regardless of what that delivery means – yes, no or not right now. In verse 9, Hannah is in the tabernacle praying and weeping. Literally, crying out and making a vow to the Lord. She promised that if the Lord were to grant her prayer, she would give the child back to Him. Although Hannah was only moving her lips and no audible words were heard by the priest, it was the weeping that got the priest, Eli's, attention. It was the weeping and the moving of her mouth that caused Eli to engage and get a better understanding of her request. It was the engaging conversation with the priest that resulted in her prayer being answered. She prayed (cried) out to God, made her request known and God moved on her behalf.

Look at God! Just like with my husband, when I want him to move, I must make my request known. Here, God knew that Hannah wanted a child, but it was not until she made her request known with a high level of urgency, coupled with the act of humbling herself in the temple before the priest, that her prayers were answered.

Again, how do we get to greater? We must get ourselves in a position where God can hear our request. Then we must provide Him with the opportunity to respond. Just like Hannah, we must humble ourselves, and then, with clarity and urgency, we must verbalize our needs and desires. By opening up to the priest she received her desire from God. The priest assured her that she would conceive and that the child would be a male! Just as she had requested.

Once God has answered our prayer, however He chooses to respond, we must react to God as He requires. We read in verse 18, after the priest informed Hannah that she would get what she asked for, "*And she said, 'Let your maidservant find favor in your sight.' So, the woman went her way and ate and her face was no longer sad*" (NKJV). Hannah left the tabernacle with a different attitude and demeanor. No longer was she sad, no longer was she in despair, no longer was she heavy-hearted. She left and she was no longer sorrowful!

Ask God, accept the response and then move forward to your next, to your greater with a different attitude. An attitude of acceptance and with the energy to do whatever is required by God.

T3:

By opening our mouths, often referred to in the Bible as crying out, we signify to God that we trust Him with the request, that we expect a response and that we trust that He will deliver regardless of what that delivery means – yes, no or not right now.

PRAYER:

Dear Lord and Answerer of Prayers,

I know that You hear my prayers and I'm thankful for Your faithfulness towards me. You continue to bless me and I will continue to give You praise for every gift.

In the giving name of Jesus,
Amen

Lord, Remember Me

When I was younger, we would sing hymns during church service. One of my favorite hymns was "He Will Remember Me." It is the story of Jesus on the cross, at Calvary, hanging between the two thieves. One thief mocked Jesus, but the other thief recognized Jesus as the Savior and asked Jesus to remember him when Jesus reached Paradise. Jesus responded in the affirmative, declaring that the thief would join Him in Paradise. The refrain of the hymn states:

"Will the Lord remember me when I am called to go? When I have crossed death's chilly sea, will He His love there show? O yes, He heard my feeble cries, from bondage He set me free. And when I reach those pearly gates He will remember me!"

Just typing those words brought excitement to my heart and tears to my eyes. Although it is a song about our transition from earth to Heaven, it does declare that once we accept the gift of salvation and recognize Jesus as our savior, there is a place reserved for us in Heaven.

The eternal memory of our God is further demonstrated through Hannah: when we make a request, in God's timing, we are remembered. Hannah illustrates that once we have humbled ourselves, cried out to God, heard the response from our Creator and changed our perspective of our situation, in due time – in His time – He will remember us. He will bless us according to His promise.

Verses 19b – 20a KJV state: *"And Elkanah knew Hannah his wife, and the Lord remembered her. So it came to pass in the process of time that Hannah conceived and bore a son..."* Look at God! He remembers! I don't know if that does anything for you, but it does everything for me. For me to know that I am not forgotten by God. Regardless of how much time passes, God has a plan for my life, and when I do as He intends and I step into the sweet spot of standing in His will for my life, where His will collides with my passion, He will remember me and bless me accordingly.

Just to know that my greater, my next level, is not stunted or disrupted by time. The knowing that if God says it, then it is so has changed my entire perspective on anything and everything happening in my life.

Really, my great*r*, once promised and ordained by God, is not dependent on Him but is totally contingent on me! I've got to get to the place where I am prepared for the greater! I'm ready for the redefinition of my life and I am accepting of the plan. Sure, I would have preferred that the peace that I am now experiencing because I have accepted God's will would have occurred earlier in my life, but it didn't. However, my greater is still on the way! Yes, I'm a bit older and I have had to live through multiple difficulties, but it ain't over and I ain't out for the count. God has made it so.

T3:

My God has remembered me! He promised it, I'm operating within it and He will give it!

PRAYER:

Dear Lord,

I understand that You are incapable of lying. Therefore, if You say it, it is so. I will believe that time is not the determiner of my receiving anything from You. It is my faith in Your promise. I choose to believe You.

In the promise keeping name of Jesus,
Amen

TELL YOUR STORY

A testimony is the sharing of a personal story that demonstrates how God operates in the life of a Believer. The testimony must give God all of the credit for the ultimate results. It shines the spotlight on the greatness of the Creator, and it can inspire others to move from where they are to where God would like them to be. When sharing my testimony, as I've confessed, I am extremely transparent. I am that way because I truly believe that through my transparency and by being authentic about my journey, I am able to help others as they travel the road back to their renewal. Most times I share without reservation. However, there are times when I wonder if I've gone too far.

During one of my speaking engagements, I shared my testimony about my not being raised in the church and how I didn't develop a true and authentic relationship with God until I was about 25 years of age. Now, I've shared this testimony many times before, but on this particular day it hit a little differently. In reading the crowd, it seemed as if many in the audience didn't approve of my late arrival to the Jesus party. The looks on their faces seemed to be judgmental, as if they were looking down on me rather than rejoicing that I did develop a relationship, regardless if it was in my 20s or not.

I started to stop sharing and change the direction of the message, but I heard a small voice telling me to continue. "Really God, that's how we're going to roll today? I'm just going to keep putting it out there without receiving any positive response?" The more I continued, the harder the stares intensified. But the voice told me to continue, and I did.

As I ended the message to a small clap of appreciation, I sat down wondering if I had done the right thing. "See God, I'm never going to be invited back!" I questioned whether or not I had helped anyone discover how awesome our God really is or whether I had just discouraged and disappointed everyone in the room. Perspiration began to build on my forehead and I dreaded having to go down into the crowd at the conclusion of the service.

Well, the benediction was completed, and it was time for me to face my consequences, go out and shake some hands. I slowly descended the pulpit and started to make my way through the crowd when I was confronted by a woman in full-out tears. All I could think was, "See Lord, look at what You made me do!" She was literally in the midst of a full-on, all-out, ugly cry. "Lord, I wasn't THAT bad, was I?" The closer she got the more nervous I got, and I noticed that she was literally shaking. As she got closer, I braced myself for the worst. She held her arms out for my embrace, so I hugged her. While hugging her I could feel her entire body shaking. She was shaking so hard that I asked someone to help me get her to a chair and I sat down with her. As we sat, she began to share with me how she too had come to the church late in life, in fact it was just recently, and she was in her 30s. She explained that she carried a lot of guilt because she felt as if God couldn't or wouldn't use her in His ministry because of her being tardy to the Jesus party. Then she shared that she needed my testimony. She needed to see me being used by God to motivate and inspire her to get engaged and to start moving toward her greater!

Just like that, I realized that my testimony of my destiny being redefined at the "late" age of 25 wasn't for everybody in that room, but that it was for that one somebody. Because I stayed the course, continued to listen and follow God's direction and chose to share my testimony of redefinition, my sister could see her *greater*. She could visualize herself being an instrument to be used by God in a way that she couldn't have conceptualized before. If I had allowed the reactions of the crowd to determine and derail my message, that woman could have missed the opportunity to experience her breakthrough. She could still be burdened by guilt and a poor self-image, resulting in others not benefiting from her participation in God's program.

That day, I learned to listen to God and to be more concerned about His opinion of me and my message and ministry and not to be bothered by the evaluation and the reactions of the crowd. Your story doesn't have to be complete, and it doesn't have to have mass appeal. It just needs to be shared. Just like Hannah sharing with Eli the priest her desperate story of being a barren woman. If she had kept it to herself, she would never have been blessed by God, and her blessing, the child Samuel, would have never been able to be used by God. As a result of Hannah sharing her story, God blessed her and the testimony of her victory is continuing to encourage others today!

Our stories have purpose. Regardless of how ugly we think our story is, how incomplete it is, or how we believe others will judge it, it still has purpose. God is the author of our testimony, and as long as He is getting the glory, our testimony will do the work that God intends. Just like Hannah, the result of our journey is a benefit of our Creator. Therefore, we must share it!

T3:

Someone's greater is contingent on the sharing of your experience. Don't hesitate. Just share.

PRAYER:

Dear Father,

I will listen to You and share my testimony. I will not be fearful and I will not be discouraged by the disapproval of the crowd. I desire to please You, so I will share. Thank You, Lord, for encouraging me to encourage others.

In the loving name of Jesus,
Amen

Be a Women of Integrity

Integrity is defined as incorruptible, an unimpaired condition. It means to do what we say we are going to do, to follow through as expected. In the redefining of who we are, moving from what people say we are and perceive us to be to where God wants us to be in thought, behavior and character, integrity is required.

In Philippians 5:11, Paul emphasizes the need for all Believers to develop a mindset like that of Jesus. That mind, the one that agreed to be the atonement for the sins of man and who, as indicated in verse 8, followed through with His intended purpose and died on the cross, not for himself but for us, is how we should operate. It is by that mind, one of integrity, that will ultimately determine our character. Jesus, a man of integrity, did what He said He would do, following through even to His death on the cross. If we are going to step into our best, into our greater, we must embrace a character that demonstrates integrity, doing what we say and have agreed to do.

In I Samuel 1:11, Hannah vowed that if God blessed her with a male child, she would give him back to God to be a servant of the Lord. After what seemed to be some hesitation from Hannah, she returned her son Samuel to the tabernacle to be used in God's service as promised. Now, I must be totally honest: when I first read the account of Samuel's birth and the vow that Hannah made and that she followed through with, I thought she was cray cray. I questioned her sanity. I mean, really. I know she promised God, but I also know all she had to endure in the process. The abuse and the ridicule that she endured because she was barren. The personal anguish that she put herself through because, although she was loved by her husband, she felt incomplete. I could feel her pain as she prayed to God to redefine her personhood. I rejoiced with her when she conceived and delivered Samuel. So that's why I couldn't understand her willingness to give her child away. I mean, really, did God expect her to honor a vow that was made out of desperation and pain?

Yes, He did and yes, He does. He expects us to operate with integrity. Because He is a God who never changes and who does what He promises, the expectation is that those who claim to follow Him must model to the world who He is. Being a person of integrity, one who is attempting to live a greater and next-level life, involves the expectation that regardless of the difficulty of the act, we will do it because we love the Lord. We are obedient to His expectations and we have faith that the result of our obedience will, first, be pleasing to Him and second, result in our experience being a blessing.

Because Hannah operated from a place of integrity and returned her son to God as she promised, she was able to experience the blessings of God in a greater, richer and deeper way. In verse 2:21, we are informed that Hannah had additional children, three sons and two daughters. It was Hannah's son, Samuel, that anointed King David and it is through that lineage that Jesus was born. Yep, that same Jesus that reconnected the lost with the Creator. Because of Hannah's integrity, her child was used by God to play a pivotal role in the life of Jesus.

If we want to get to our better, our next level and our greater, it is necessary to have integrity. We must do what we say we're going to do so that we make way for God to include us in a larger part of His program.

T3:

To get to the next level of greater you must honor your promises to demonstrate your readiness. To prove that you are trustworthy.

PRAYER:

Dear Lord,

I desire to be more like You. If I say it, promise it, then it can be considered done. I will honor You with my integrity. I will demonstrate that I've been faithful with the smaller things and I am ready for the next.

In the trustworthy name of Jesus,
Amen

REVIVE:

To regain life, consciousness or strength

Widow of Nain: Luke 7:11 – 17

The widowed mother of one son living in Nain. She experiences the compassion of Jesus.

JESUS SEES YOU

In these scriptures, the main character doesn't have a name and, seemingly, has a very bleak future. All that we know is that she is a widow from Nain that has just lost her only son. She's nameless and being described by her very desperate circumstances. Why is her situation so bleak? Because during Biblical times a widowed woman was expected to be cared for by her eldest male child. As you can see, her only son has died. Even though the scriptures indicate that she's in a crowd, I can only imagine that she is feeling all alone and concerned about her next steps. How will she live? How will she be cared for? What does her future look like? Yes, she's in a crowd of well-meaning people, but none of these people are responsible for her future, her tomorrow.

I don't know if you've ever been there. Being amid a crowd of people but knowing that none of the crowd can truly "see" the insecurities that lie within. They see you but they really don't "see" you. They see your presence – your physical stature, your smile, your fashion sense. They hear your conversation – the lightness in your voice, the words you speak, your tone and tempo of speech. They even receive the love that you are willing to share. But they don't see into the depths of your soul. They don't see what is hidden behind the smile, the pain that is covered by the clothes, the tears that are masked by the inflection of your voice. What you project is confidence, coolness, power and authority. It seems to those looking in that you are ready for greater and you are assuredly on the road to the next level. Shoot, many may believe you've already arrived. All the while, you are shaking in your designer shoes, doubting what God has for you, wondering if you're prepared and feeling as if you are an imposter. Wait! This is starting to feel like it's getting personal.

I've lived most of my life in the space of being insecure. Yes, I've experienced some moments when I've known beyond a shadow of a doubt that I was in my best space. That I was operating fully on all cylinders. That level of confidence usually shows up when I am operating in my gifts. When I'm sharing God's word, in that moment, I'm good. However, after all is said and done, after I've said my last amen, after I've taught the last point of a lesson, after I've closed the computer from studying for the day, I quickly spiral into being overwhelmed with the need to cover and mask my insecurities. I fake like I'm all good and that I've got it all together. I am a habitual hider from people. I do not allow people to see me for who and what I really am, an insecure imposter.

Yes, I struggle with confidence. As I pen the words of this book, doing something that I've never done before but feel compelled to do because I believe it is in God's will, I am shaking with each punch of each computer key. Yep, I fully understand the widow, in a crowd but all alone. Having to reconcile her present reality with her future of uncertainty.

But look at Jesus! Talk about being able to "see" you. He sees your need and He has the power and the authority to change the trajectory of your future in an instant. Jesus, without asking questions, could see the condition of the widow's heart and her soul and He moved in compassion to get her to her next, to her greater. He saw the heaviness that seemed to cripple her potential! With just a touch, He removed it all!

That's how our God works! He can see your deepest concerns, doubts and fears. He looks beyond the image that we attempt to portray, and He gets us in the space where we can be catapulted to our greater. He moves us beyond our fears by removing barriers and obstacles. He provides us with all that is necessary to get to where He needs us to be.

Where does He need us to be? In the space of greater, confidently!

T3:

Even when we are standing in a place of doubt, hesitation and insecurity we must lean on the One who can and will change our situation, immediately. Our God compassionately and completely "sees" us, and He maps the directions for our travel to get us to our greater!

PRAYER:

Dear God,

Your compassion fuels our travels to get us to the sweet spot where our passions collide with Your will. It is in that space that we will find our greater. We thank you, Father, for Your compassion and love and for Your touch that heals all that ails us.

In the compassionate name of Jesus,
Amen

It Ain't About the Crowd

When I was younger, I remember watching sporting events, music concerts and even church services on television. I was amazed by the number of people who were in the stands and the congregations – the spectators. What seemed to mesmerize me the most was watching the church services. Don't ask me why it was so interesting to me because I wasn't really a churchgoer, as I've previously explained. I mean, I attended church, but it was sporadic. Honestly, I'm still unsure why I would be glued to the tube watching all the activity, the preacher reading the scriptures, pounding his fist on the podium and on the Bible, raising and lowering his voice. Most of the people in the crowd seemed to be holding onto every single word, responding with the appropriate and well placed "Amen" and "Hallelujah." It was truly amazing. I was astounded by how the preacher had such command of the crowd and how the crowd was just waiting for the next opportunity to articulate their agreement.

As I got older and really became part of a congregation, I would think back to those times, watching the services on TV. I would watch to see if my pastor had command of the crowd like the TV preacher. Watching as the congregation would look for opportunities to say "Amen" and "Hallelujah." Watching as my pastor orchestrated a well-crafted word that would excite the congregation and lead them into a riotous celebration.

But what I also observed was that once the service was over, once my pastor would shake the last hand and smile at the last baby, he would return to his office and sit in his chair – alone. He was left without the crowd, without all the positive affirmations of the people, left alone without the shouts of agreement or the encouraging pats on the back. He was left with just himself, his personal evaluation of his message and his thoughts about whether or not he'd pleased God.

One Sunday, I asked him about how that felt, to have the large crowd seeming to be with him and seeming to be moved by the message and the ministry, only to have to return to his office alone. What he shared was this:

- Although the people are shouting their praise, it doesn't indicate that they are truly understanding the point of the message.
- Those same people who are shouting their approval in the sanctuary are the same people who go home and criticize you behind your back.
- That he is always concerned about whether or not what was intended by the sermon was what the people received, and –

Here's what I found to be most important:

- He never looks for the approval of man, but he strives to please God.

- It isn't about the approval of the crowd; it is about the effectiveness of the message. He would rather they not say a thing but walk away changed and transformed, and
- It is necessary for him to remain focused on God, His will and His intentions.

To say that I was floored would be an understatement. See, I was focused on the crowd and their approval. My pastor redirected my attention to the true purpose of ministry, God's glory and the people's transformation. In Galatians 1:10, the Apostle Paul reminds us to keep the main thing the main thing. Don't get caught up trying to be approved by man. As Believers, our focus is to make God smile! I regularly remind my Sunday school class that my goal is to have God look over the side of Heaven, see me and smile!

The Biblical story of the Widow of Nain reveals that although she was in a crowd, her attention wasn't on the crowd. Her attention was, firstly, on her hopeless situation. But her focus was moved from her hopeless present to her victorious future. She experienced Jesus by redirecting her focus and was able to claim the victorious blessing that He was prepared and willing to give her. Her attitude and disposition were transformed into gratitude and praise.

If we are going to get to our greater, we must concentrate on the correct assessor of our work. The success of our work is not determined by size of the crowd. The success of our greater is determined by whether or not the giver of our calling is pleased by our work. Because when the crowd dissipates and you are left to solitude, loneliness or lonesomeness, the only "Well done!" that matters is the one given by the Father.

T3:

Don't get caught up trying to be approved by man. As Believers, our focus is to make God smile!

PRAYER:

Dear God,

I will seek Your approval. I will remain focused on You and Your will. It is for You that I live and have my purpose. Thank You for using me in the building of Your Kingdom.

In the name of Jesus,
Amen

DRY YOUR TEARS

Tears have their benefits. They:

- Release toxins that may be stored in the body
- Keep the eyes from getting too dry, thus improving your vision
- By fighting bacteria that could cause loss of sight by cleansing the eyes
- Relieve stress
- Can counteract pain by releasing endorphins that change people's mood
- Help a person self-soothe, and
- Indicate to others that someone may be in need of help.

This is all good! But tears can stagnate our progress and our growth. If we remain focused on the pain that is generating the tears, we can miss the opportunity to access needed help and to reengage in our journey. We become focused on the pain rather than concentrating on the promise. Hey, that was good! I'll say that again: We become so focused on the pain, rather than concentrating on the promise, that we miss something that God is doing in our lives. Because we are so engrossed in activity that doesn't serve us in moving to our greater, we lose precious time and opportunity – we become tired and overwhelmed. It is at those times that we open ourselves up to become victims rather than victors. We lose opportunities to access our God-promised abundant living. The abundant living that is the product of our being in the sweet spot where passion meets calling, the spot where God is pleased with our representation and our work.

I truly believe that our humanistic tendency to remain in a paralyzed condition, with our vision obscured by the tears generated by our pain, is a tactic used by the enemy to keep us from getting to our greater and from participating fully in our God-graced purpose. Now, I am not discounting pain, because it's real. Throughout God's word, we are warned that trials, tribulations and difficulties are to be expected. In fact, we are informed that we must put on the whole amour of God so that we can endure the fiery darts of the enemy. So, the existence of pain is genuine. However, our God is bigger than any pain, plot or pitfall generated by our enemies. He desires to demonstrate His power and authority over everything, using us, His children, as the instrument and an example to the world!

That's why David, in Psalm 30 KJV, repeatedly reminds the reader that our God is a keeper of His promises, an answerer of prayers and a restorer of His people. Whatever we are going through, God is forever reminding us, through sometimes very small things, that He has promised us better and that He will fulfill His promise. In verse 5, David reminds us that *"weeping* (tears) *may endure for a night, but* (I love this conjunction because it indicates an override of the previous statement!) *joy comes in the morning."* It exhorts us to remain focused on the promises of God.

It's human for us to get sidetracked and to lose focus on what God has told us to be true. It is during those difficult times that we need to speak to ourselves, dry our tears and lean on the Lord of our lives. We have a work to do and a greater to get to; we cannot and must not allow the tears of today to obscure the greatness of our tomorrow.

When we are confronted with situations that cause us pain and could potentially derail us, we must do as Jesus instructs in Luke 7:13 AMP: *"Do not weep."* So get that facial tissue, dry those tears, recalibrate and continue your journey – revived! Revived with a new excitement and spirit of commitment and a laser focus on your calling and your greater!

T3:

We have a work to do and a greater to get to; we cannot and must not allow the tears of today to obscure the greatness of our tomorrow.

PRAYER:

Dear Lord,

I am leaning on You to dry my tears so that I can keep it moving toward my greater, my bigger, my better and my abundance. I will focus on Your greatness and Your mighty power, knowing that You are bigger and mightier than anything that may come against me. I appreciate Your continued protection.

In the protective name of Jesus,
Amen

STOP!

I tend to be someone who, once I get started, has to go full steam ahead! I start running down the track of getting it done. Checking off items on my list, making calls, building relationships, all the things. I will run, run, run until it is done. I get so focused on the stuff, on the things, that I lose sight of the true purpose. Sometimes, because of all of the doing, I forget what God originally wanted for me to do – the calling that He has for me: my greater. I'm looking with satisfaction on the items completed, never assessing whether the intended purpose for the work is being achieved. Am I assisting anyone in their transformation? Am I helping anyone to get to their greater? Am I making investments or just spinning my wheels? What I've come to understand is that completion doesn't mean progress. Just because it has a check mark next to it doesn't mean that it has hit God's intended target.

Here's the heart-breaking part! All the while we are getting things done and checking items off our list, our effectiveness in our calling and the progression of our journey to greatness is dying or is already dead. Just like the son of the Widow of Nain was dead, our progress to our greater is dead. The difference is the widow knew and understood that her hope for her future lay dead in that casket and needed a miracle to revive her possibilities. We, on the other hand, can get so engrossed in the tasks that we don't even realize the ultimate purpose, and our progress is dying or dead. We don't realize until that one morning when we wake up exhausted, unmotivated, lost, unsure and unsteady. At that moment, our insecurities rise and we don't know how or even why we should move forward. We don't even take the moment to pray because we are despondent and disconnected from our power source. So, we just get up and do only what we know to do, whatever is next on the list. Lost, dead and despondent!

However, the scriptures tell us just what to do in those moments. For us to be revived and to refocus, we must stop chasing accomplishments and incline our ears and our attention to the One that has the power and the authority to revive our hope, our passion and our purpose. We must turn our attention away from our *"to do lists"* and toward the sustainer of our strength. Verse 14 AMP says *"those that were carrying him stood still."* The carriers of the dead purpose, dead focus, dead vision and dead possibilities stopped. Just STOP!

Yep! Just stop, listen and refocus. Listen to the instructions and watch God get to work. The pallbearers stopped, and because of their obedience, they were able to witness Jesus perform a miraculous work of revival. New hope, new possibilities, new focus and new energy.

They stopped and Jesus started. What was once dead is now alive, and greater is still possible. Stopping doesn't mean stagnation! Stopping provides opportunity for reenergization. Sometimes progress requires us to stop, be still and watch our God do His mighty work.

T3:

For us to be revived and to refocus, we must stop chasing accomplishments and incline our ears and our attention to the One who has the power and the authority to revive our hope, our passion and our purpose.

PRAYER:

Father God,

I love how You give me the opportunity to STOP, regroup and refocus. Continue to remind me that it ain't about checking off the list. Your work is about transformation, and that takes time.

In the patient name of Jesus,
Amen

IT AIN'T OVER

Since I've been writing this section, Revive, the song by Maurette Brown Clark, "It Ain't Over," keeps bouncing around in my head,

> I know the odds look stacked against you
> And it seems there's no way out
> I know the issue seems unchangeable
> And that there's no reason to shout
> But the impossible is God's chance
> To work a miracle, a miracle
> So just know
> It ain't over until God says it's over
> It ain't over until God says it's done
> It ain't over until God says it's over
> Keep fighting until your victory is won

This is an encouragement to the Believer and to the journeyman who is seeking to honor the will of God for our lives. It informs us to look beyond what seems to be the realistic outcome of a situation and begin to focus on the fact that this is an opportunity for God to work in our lives, miraculously! How awesome is that?!

Just as the Widow of Nain was thinking that her fate was sealed and that from that day forward her living was going to be difficult and challenging, Jesus stepped in and totally blew everyone's mind. Can you imagine? A funeral procession, interrupted by a miracle, is transformed into a party of praise! The widow was focused on loss. Loss of her son. Loss of her lifestyle. Loss of her options. Her focus is on her problems and her pain. But, because God has a purpose for everything that we encounter and because He majors in what seems to be impossible, now she must change her thinking, her plans and her actions to embrace the potentials. All because Jesus saw her. He was moved by compassion, and she was rescued and her greater was revived.

Here's what is also so amazing: the response of the crowd. She was standing in the midst of them, but they couldn't fully share in her devastating situation. That crowd of onlookers? They are no longer the witnesses of a sad story to be told from a position of sympathy, empathy and pain. They are now witnesses of what can happen if we just stop, listen, get out of the way and allow our God to do His revival work! Can you just imagine the stories that were told? The stories of triumph and victory. The stories of the power and authority of our God. The testimonies of standing still and allowing God to do what God does best – the miraculous! So, I believe that not only has the future of the widow changed, but also the futures of those in the crowd. The widow's blessing is now a blessing that impacts the community!

Now, are you seeing what I'm seeing? If we just stop and allow the God that knows us and sees us to do the miraculous in our lives, we can be a blessing and a testimony to others. To those who have looked at your situation and counted you out, they must now tell the story about how you allowed God to step in, show up and show out. That your sad story is now a testimony of the goodness and greatness of our God.

Yep! It ain't over!

As Maurette Brown Clark's song continues,

> When people say you can't, remember
> (He can, He will)
> When you don't know what you're gonna do,
> Please remember
> (He has the master plan)
> He will free you from your sin
> And give you peace within
> So you better hold your head up high
> You're gonna win
> (You're gonna win)

T3:

If we just stop and allow the God who knows us and sees us to do the miraculous in our lives and revive that which seemed to be dead, our experience will be a blessing and a testimony to others.

PRAYER:

Dear Lord,

Allow my difficulties to be a testimony to the world about Your power and Your glory. Use me to demonstrate that what seems impossible to man is an opportunity for You to do what only You can.

In the name of the one who is the source of possibilities, Jesus,

Amen

LISTEN

In the development of our prayer life, only half of it is talking to God. The other, and most important, half is the listening for God's response. Listening for His instructions and expectations. For us to get to our greater, to live within the will of God, to be in the sweet spot, we are required to listen.

I know everyone has either read or heard about studies that illustrate how little we actually listen when in conversation. In fact, when I was in preschool, we played a game where the teacher would whisper something in the ear of a classmate and the classmate would then whisper it to the next person. This would continue until we got to the last person in the circle. The last person would then say out loud what was told to them. It never failed that what was told at the end of the circle is not at all what was said at the beginning. Often, it is so far from where the story started that it is confusing as to where the alterations actually occurred. The reason the story changes is because humans have difficulty listening.

It's like when you are in a discussion with your mate. Man, sometimes that is the most difficult time to listen. Why? Because we are not concentrating on what is being said! Our attention is on our comeback or it is on what we want to hear rather than on what was actually said!

That's exactly what we do to God. We tell God something, make a request, look for direction, look for clarity – but we never stop and wait for a response. Then we begin to formulate the next thing that we want to say. Forming our response based on incomplete and inaccurate information. This leads to lost opportunity, unnecessary falls and trips and much confusion and pain.

Here in Luke 7, we see the necessity of developing the art of listening to the Father. Listening so that we can maintain our focus and receive the revival that we may need from time to time. In verse 13, Jesus tells the widow to stop weeping. Just think what that did for her. It changed her focus from her impossible and desperate situation, and she was able to witness what only God could make possible. In verse 14, the pallbearers listened, and they stood still. Because they listened and obeyed, they were able to become witnesses of the power and authority of Jesus. They got to see His authority even over death. In verse 14, the dead boy listened, and he was revived.

But look, that's not all. Verse 17 states that the testimony of the miracle went out to all of Judea and all of the surrounding region. Now, if those that HEAR the testimony of the reviving power of Jesus make the decision to follow Him, to get into the will of the Father, what victories they will be able to experience! What joy they will be able to possess! What peace they will become familiar with, because they now can begin the journey to their greatness! Just because they listened.

In our journey to greatness, the development of the skill of listening is essential to our avoiding many unnecessary barriers and pitfalls along the path. If we listen, we will receive the revival that we occasionally need along the journey. If we just be still and just listen, our greatness and our usefulness will be a testimony to the power and the love of our Creator.

T3:

Stop talking and listen!

PRAYER:

Dear Lord,

My ears are inclined toward You, Lord. Give me directions and I will follow.

In the precious name of Jesus,
Amen

PRAISE IS NECESSARY

Periodically, I will do an assessment of my journey, evaluating if I am remaining within the will of God and whether I am meeting the expectations that He has for me. In all honesty, I have missed the mark on more occasions than I care to admit.

There have been times that I seem to be right in line with what God intends. As I am completing my assessment, it is during those times, times when I am in alignment with God, when things seem to be easier. Not less difficult. No fewer trials or tribulations. But I am more at peace with whatever is occurring in my life at that time. When I am in stride with God.

However, there are other times in my life where I seem to be totally out of alignment. Just like a car, I have hit a bump in the road, and now I'm bearing too much to one side or the other. It's a struggle to stay straight. I realize that I am expending more energy in just trying to stay straight. I'm just maintaining; not making any significant progress. It is during my assessment that I attempt to figure out what happened, what caused my spiritual alignment to get all out of whack.

What I've come to discover is that it can be a few things:

- My lack of focus on those things that God has promised,
- My reluctance to just stop and let God be God,
- My inability to trust that God's got me and even though it may look like it's over, it ain't, or
- I haven't been listening to God and then being obedient to His direction.

However, there's another reason that my spiritual alignment gets out of whack. This reason is often missed by people because it's not natural human behavior. It is contradictory to what we have experienced and to our character. What is it? It's the giving of praise to my God! Yep, I forget to give God praise! I'm not talking about just the emotional nondescriptive praise. I'm talking about deep-down-in-my-soul praise for the specifics of how God has operated on my behalf. The kind of praise that indicates to God my sincere appreciation for what He has done, is doing and will do. It is the type of praise that is intentional and intelligent; not just generated by emotions. It is thoughtful praise.

See, sometimes we become so accustomed to the goodness of God that we begin to take it for granted. We begin to envision God as our hired help. That God is here to meet our needs. Therefore, we don't have to praise Him for the wonderful blessings He gives us because that's what He's supposed to do. We get so self-absorbed that we neglect to see and appreciate the faithfulness and love of our God. It is in those moments of neglect that we slowly get out of alignment with God and are forced to rediscover and reappreciate how special our spiritual relationship is.

Luke 7:16 AMP states, "*The fear* (meaning reverence) *came upon all, and they GLORIFIED God, saying, 'A great prophet has risen up among us'; and, 'God has visited His people."* I hope you see it. Not only did the widow praise God for what He had done for her, but the entire crowd praised God for who He is in the personality of Jesus. They praised Him because they'd gotten the opportunity to experience Him as He blessed another.

Praise is necessary. The recognition of the awesomeness of God is required. Look at this: we must recognize and glorify Him not because of what He does for us only. We should praise Him just for who He is and what He is doing in the lives of others.

T3:

As you journey on your path to greatness, don't forget to have an authentic and intelligent praise break along the way.

Prayer:

Dear Lord,

I praise You for who You are. That is all.

In the awesome name of Jesus,
Amen

REPLENISH:

FILL UP AGAIN, RESTORE TO A FORMER LEVEL OR CONDITION

Woman with the issue of blood
(Matthew 9:20 – 22; Mark 5:25 – 34
and Luke 8:43 – 48):

A nameless woman who was suffering with a continuous hemorrhaging of blood for 12 years. She is mentioned in three of the gospels, Matthew, Luke and Mark.

Consider the Source

This is an extremely familiar passage of scripture that is often used to demonstrate the necessity of faith in our eventual healing and restoration. However, what always seems to get my attention is the fact that this woman had tried other remedies and had been unsuccessful but maintained her desire to be healed.

Have you ever wanted something so badly that you looked for it to come from varied tried sources? I remember desiring love and companionship so deeply in my younger years that I looked for it in multiple forms. I would latch onto friends, looking to have a confidante to share my most intimate secrets with. These relationships lasted for periods of time but would often result in disappointment and pain. Or I looked for companionship in the form of romantic relationships. These relationships would start out all hot and heavy, neither ever wanting to be out of each other's presence, only to fizzle out within a few short months or even a few years. With the fizzling came regret, remorse, grief and sometimes guilt. I kept looking, looking for someone to fill the empty spaces so that I could feel worthy and complete. Worthy of being connected to. Really worthy of being loved and accepted. Let's just say that this period of my life was not filled with very many shining moments.

The sad thing is, with each disappointment, each failed relationship and each betrayal of trust, I developed a mentality that it was better to stop searching and just accept being alone. I vowed to end my search and just find peace in my singleness. Not just singleness in a romantic sense, but singleness in my attachments, of all types!

Here's the thing: I never really took a moment to consider the source. I never considered that I was looking for acceptance and companionship from a source that couldn't really fill me like I desired or needed. I was making unreasonable demands of people who could never rise to that responsibility. Honestly, when I look back, I see that none of those individuals ever wanted to be placed in that role in the first place. I put them there when they were never qualified to meet the expectations. I was expecting them to complete me. I think I remember that from a movie, but anyway, how unrealistic is that? Expecting someone to make you whole. To heal you and to fill your cup, so to speak, when most times they themselves are operating from an empty cup!

No one should be burdened with the responsibility of making you feel worthy, confident and whole. That is too heavy a burden for anyone to have to bear. The unfortunate thing is that I continued to believe in the fallacy that someone could complete me. I looked for someone to be my source of security and fulfillment until I had been so damaged that I became more and more detached and despondent.

Then, when I was reading this passage, it dawned on me: I was looking to the wrong well from which to quench my thirst. Yep, if you are a Generation Z, I was what you all call thirsty. What I needed to do was to reconsider the source. Mark 5 indicates that the woman had already sought out sources that were professionals and were expected to have the ability to heal illnesses of the body. I love the Mark 5 version because it showed the extent to which she had gone to be healed. In fact, she had spent all of her financial resources trying to be healed. But, eventually, she took a moment and considered the source. Where could she most assuredly be healed? Who had the authority and the power to truly restore her – completely? Who is the one true source that loves her so much and desires to bless her with the desires of her heart? Where is it that she can find what she is searching for?

Once she heard about Jesus, she determined that her greater was where He was. Her next-level living was within His power. He possessed the ability to give her what she was searching for and to make her whole. She would be able to be greater because the burden would be lifted and her bondage would be broken. It would be Jesus who would support her movement from brokenness to fulfillment. From being shattered to being whole. From being described and categorized by her inadequacies to being victorious and blessed. Because she considered the source and redirected her hopes to the correct source, she was able to move beyond her limitations to the fullness of her possibilities.

T3:

No one should be burdened with the responsibility of making you feel worthy, confident and whole. Only God has the power and the authority to restore and revive - completely.

PRAYER:

Lord,

You are the source of my healing and the well where I will quench my thirst. It is through You that I am made whole.

In the complete name of Jesus,
Amen

REACH UP

There are times in our lives, more often than we care to admit, when we are just tapped out. Being honest, even when we are operating in our calling, standing in alignment with God and demonstrating our God-given gifts, we still experience moments when we don't believe we can move another further, take another step or do another thing. On top of doing and being in our sweet spot, we must still participate in the other varied demands of life: maintaining our homes, going to work, fulfilling obligations that weigh us down and pull on every resource in our reserve. We are just plain tired, and we feel as if no one knows, cares or understands.

As I am writing, I am coming out of a moment just like this, when I was running on empty – just running on fumes! During the previous four weeks, I have hosted, in my town, my three-day family reunion that we'd been planning for about eight months; taken my daughter to college, which is more than twelve hours away (yep, we drove a Honda Accord that was filled to the roof with all her things); moved her into her dorm, which was an ALL DAY EVENT; and flew home so that my husband (who is the president of our state convention for churches) could kick off the annual session (which required me to attend because I am a dutiful partner in the ministry) – all while needing to find some quiet time to continue to write. On top of those things, I was responsible for meeting some very important deadlines at work, hosting an annual meeting that was the culmination of over two years of some extremely difficult but important work, and preparing for the departure of a staff member to make sure that none of their work responsibilities fell through the cracks! To say that I was depleted in all areas of my life –mentally, physically and spiritually – would be an understatement! I was totally and completely exhausted.

Again, I read Mark 5 about this woman, the woman with the issue of blood. In my moment of depletion, God highlighted for me my answer. He informed me about what I needed so that I could be refilled, regain my strength and continue on my journey. I needed to reach up!

Here's the key: I couldn't reach out. Grasping for anything that I thought could meet my need. I needed to reach up for the specific Someone. I needed someone who had the power and the authority to heal me and to refill me. Yep, I needed to reach up! Reach up to Jesus so that I could actually feel Him and invite Him to do what He does best – restore. But, what is most important is that when I – when we – reach up, we must do so with the absolute confidence that He will restore. No wavering in our belief in His power and in His authority. Just like He told the woman with all of her issues, because she had faith, she was healed and made whole. Because she had faith that He was the One that she needed and that He was the only one who could meet the need, she was healed.

So when we've done all we can and we feel like we have reached the end of our rope, don't tie a knot and hold on. Reach up with confidence to the supplier of our strength and then return to the work. Return healed, return complete and return whole.

T3:

When we are depleted, we must reach up to Jesus so we can actually feel Him and invite Him to do what He does best – restore.

PRAYER:

Dear Lord,

You are the source of my strength! Remind me to reach up and not out!

In the replenishing name of Jesus,
Amen

BREAK THE RULES

There will always be something or someone who will attempt to block you from completely and wholly engaging in your calling. It could be people, illnesses, rules, policies, customs, norms, self-imposed restrictions, self-doubt, lack of resources or confidence – anything. The unfortunate thing is, we will allow all of those things to step in our way and divert us from moving to the place where God wants us to be or where we can be used by Him. We will allow those things to block us from our blessings and from putting us in a place where we can be a blessing to others. We allow, give permission to and provide space to those things that hamper our peace and our fulfillment. We make space for those things that add weight to our wings and hamper our ascension to greater and higher. We hamper our greater because we don't tap into the resources that will get us to the place and the space that will permit us to operate fully in our calling, our sweet spot. We don't tap into the greater that lives within. Therefore, we miss the opportunities to live out loud in our space of greatness, boldly!

Because we allow the "things" to block us, we tie God's hands, so to speak, from pouring out the fullness of His blessings and from using us as He intended. But here's the thing: we *allow* this to occur. Yep, we give those things permission to paralyze us and to hamper us. We give the blockers space, resulting in our greatness being outside of our reach. Yep, we can't envision the greatness that our God has for us because we are too concerned with those things that limit us and obscure our possibilities.

It was Jewish law that when a woman was bleeding, she was not to be around other people. In fact, she was considered unclean, and if someone touched her, they too would become unclean, requiring them to go through a ceremonial cleansing. So, women who were experiencing this type of bleeding would quarantine themselves until their flow was complete. Do you realize what that meant for this woman? She needed to be in quarantine for 12 years. She needed to navigate her life so that she remained isolated from others. She had to continually be conscious of the possibility of contaminating others and thereby inhibiting them from living their lives fully. She couldn't be great because she was blocked by her physical aliment and the rules that governed her behaviors. Therefore, she was confined, imprisoned and alone – blocked by laws that hampered her possibilities and her opportunities.

But she had reached her end. The end of her resources, the end of her patience, the end of her tolerance to endure what I'm sure was intolerable. She decided to ignore those things that blocked her and to get to the One who could heal her and unlock the door to her greatness! She was going to get to the One who would give her a chance to step into her life fully and completely. I'm sure she didn't know what to expect, but what I know for sure is that she didn't allow the unforeseeable to hinder her possibilities.

This is what I love about this woman. I don't care what it took for her to jump out on faith and get her deliverance; she did it and she did it fearlessly. Now, I'm not saying she didn't experience fear. I'm saying that she did what was necessary to move from bondage to freedom and that she did it despite of her fear! She did not allow anything to stand in the way of her greatness. Not rules, not customs, not people, not the crowd and not even her fear!

For us to step into our greatness, we've got to move beyond those things that may get in our way so that we can maintain our connection with Jesus and our internal power. It is that power that will propel us to the next space and place. Darn the rules and embrace the greatness that is on the beyond, on the other side!

T3:

We can't envision the greatness that our God has for us because we are too concerned with those things that limit us and obscure our possibilities. Don't do that!

PRAYER:

Dear Lord,

Don't let me be obstructed from my greatness by anything. Not rules, not customs, not policies, not people and not my own fears. Help me to develop a spirit of faith over my fears.

In the fearless name of Jesus,
Amen

By Any Means Necessary

In the previous reading, I highlighted the fact that barriers and challenges will present themselves as we move from where we are to where God desires us to be. For us to get to our greatness, we need to tap into the internal power, the God within, that will propel us to the next. The next place where God will use us and prepare us for the more. The thing is, to do this – to tap into the power of our God and get to greatness – will require us to be single-minded and laser focused on God's will and His desire. We've got to develop a determination where we know that we know that we know that God intends for us to experience more. He intends for us to be more. It is with this laser focus and our shift from what we can see to what we can't (but what we understand to be true because God has placed it deep within) that we will continue to cooperate with God. Cooperate to the point where we do what we never believed or conceived that we would or could. To be great and do great, to get beyond the obstacles that will present themselves in our journey, we have to develop a "by any means necessary" mentality and focus.

Look at this woman, the one with the issue, the one that was defined by her inabilities rather than by her potential. The woman who seemed to be down and by all definitions should have been out. This woman, the one who was quarantined, left alone and without resources. This woman who was seen by everyone who knew her as handicapped and unable to live a full life. She determined within herself that she was no longer going to be withheld by the chains that bound her. She was going to engage in a prison break. In order to be free, that break required that she use drastic, unconventional and dangerous measures. She was going to be free to be greater and to experience her next.

In Luke's depiction of this event, the woman touches the hem, the border or the tassels of His garment. By any means necessary! Firstly, she had to determine that she was going to risk being in the crowd and jeopardizing the cleanliness of the community that would come within her proximity. Potentially facing persecution and shame. She even had to acknowledge her fear and still do what was necessary for her to gain her freedom.

But here's the thing: Once she got to the space where Jesus was, she had to get to Him, she had to get to His personhood. That required her to get down and reach up. Get down so that she could be made whole. Get down so that she could get past all that stood between her and her getting to greater. Get down so that she could just touch a part of Him so that He could heal her. She needed and wanted to be restored, to be reenergized, to be replenished. But for that to happen, she had to get down. Down to her lowest point. Not only was she depleted of her financial resources, she was also depleted of anything that would get in her way of being replenished. She knew the rules, she knew the norms, she knew the risk, but she had to do whatever was necessary to get to her greater. Forget the rules, forget the potential persecution, forget the potential punishment and move past her fear.

So, with her "by any means necessary" mentality, she got down and touched His hem. She got in His proximity, she humbled herself, she reached up and she was made whole!

For us to be used by God and to be able to access our completeness and our greatness, we will be required to develop a "by any means" mentality. Even if we have to fall down so that we can be lifted, so be it! We have to determine from within that the risk is worth our getting to our greater!

T3:

A "by any means necessary" mentality says even if we have to fall down so that we can be lifted, so be it!

Prayer:

Dear Lord,

I want to be whole so that I can step into my sweet spot of passion + calling and being used for Your purpose. By any means necessary, I am determined to get into Your space, thus getting to my greater.

In the unyielding name of Jesus,
Amen

Rock Bottom is a New Beginning

We fall down
But we get up
We fall down
But we get up
We fall down
But we get up
For a saint
Is just a sinner who fell down,
But we couldn't stay there,
And got up

These are the words from a familiar song sung by Donnie McClurkin and released in 2000, "We Fall Down." What I envision whenever I hear these words is one of God's disciples, a follower of Christ, who has fallen short, has experienced a spiritual setback. He/she has hit the proverbial rock bottom.

As I stated earlier, my true and genuine journey with Christ did not start until I was 25 years of age. Now, to be clear, I knew who Jesus was and understood the role that He served in the life of a

Believer. I'd even spent time attending church. I was a faithful CME member. No, not the denomination; *CME* – Christmas, Mother's Day and Easter church attendee. If I wasn't at church at any other time, I was there on those very special and significant days. But, when I finally accepted Christ as my Savior and my Lord, I struggled with who I was versus who God expected me to become. I couldn't find my way, clearly, now that I was a new creation. Yep, I heard all the words, but I wasn't able to actualize them in my mind. My mind was stuck in the paradigm of what I was, and it was difficult for me to make the shift to what I was becoming. I couldn't conceive how I was going to live out my greatness as God intended.

See, from a very early age, I understood that I was not utilizing all of my talents, skills and abilities. I was not operating in my full potential. Because of that mindset, whenever I would fall short or miss the mark, I would wallow in self-pity and spend precious moments beating myself up and rebuking myself for falling down – again. I was forever in a state of rock bottom. Never freeing myself of unrealistic expectations. Continually, I would block myself from the space and place that would support my being greater. I didn't fall down; I lived down. Down was my permanent address.

Since I dwelled in a permanent space of rock bottom, I did not give God space to forgive me, heal me or lift me. I fell down, lived down and could not see myself in any other way than down. But it was in this state of brokenness that I read, I mean really *read*, the words in Romans 8:38 and 39 NLT: *"And I am convinced that nothing can ever separate us from God's love. Neither death nor life, neither angels nor demons, neither our fears for today nor our worries about tomorrow—not even the powers of hell can separate us from God's love. No power in the sky above or in the earth below—indeed, nothing in all creation will ever be able to separate us from the love of God that is revealed in Christ Jesus our Lord."*

Wait, you mean to tell me that nothing or nobody, not even myself, can separate me from the love that God has for me? Even with all my mistakes and wretchedness, He still loves me. Despite it all, He still cares. Regardless of my living at rock bottom, He still desires to use me for His glory. My greatness is not withdrawn by God. I can't embarrass God enough so that He would leave me at rock bottom and not allow me to get back up. Here's the best part, as Donnie repeats in his song several times over: Get back up again!

I've come to understand that on my journey to live out the greatness that God has poured into me for the purpose of bringing Him glory, I will fall and I will hit rock bottom. But it is at rock bottom that I can hear God, embrace His teachings and expectations, apply them to my life and start, not all over, but anew.

T3:

A new beginning is at your rock bottom.

PRAYER:

Dear Lord,

I know that rock bottom may be necessary for my getting to great. I thank You for not leaving me there and for allowing me to get back up again.

In the compassionate name of Jesus,
Amen

SPEAK UP!

Shame and fear are powerful in their ability to stagnate and prevent us from getting to the place where we can be used by God for the purpose of kingdom building. If I haven't made it clear by now, your greatness is not for you to be able to sit in comfort and enjoy the ancillary benefits of your connection with God without using those God-given benefits beyond yourself. Your greatness is intended to glorify God and to add to the kingdom. Period! My husband often says that the only thing that you can take to Heaven with you is other people. All the stuff that you gather and accumulate can't go. When you transition, the stuff remains. People are the only thing that can transition with you, and the reason that God wants to use you is so that you can inspire and attract others to want to come with you.

You should have an "I can't help it" attitude when it comes to this work. I can't help doing the work. I can't help engaging with God's creation for His glory. I can't help wanting to satisfy God. I can't help wanting to live at the highest level and desiring to bring a smile to the face of God. I've got to live by the principle that God's pleasure is my ultimate goal.

Unfortunately, shame and fear will hamper us from implementing the game plan and doing the work. Part of the work is sharing our story with others. Helping others to see the benefits and the freedom that we all experience once we align our lives with the will of the Father. Our stories, as I've said before, are necessary for others to connect with the possibilities of God and allow them to see themselves being connected to Him. They need to see themselves differently to give themselves permission to step into His presence. But we have got to share our testimony by moving past the shame and the fear.

After the woman, the broken woman, with the issue of blood, in the midst of the crowd, touched Jesus, He asked who touched Him. In the midst of all those people in the crowd, Jesus asked who touched Him? Now, let's be clear: Jesus was fully aware of who touched Him. We must always be conscious of the fact that God uses every experience – every up, every down, every encounter, ever moment that you go through – for the purpose of demonstrating His love, power and authority to the people. Here, He uses the testimony of the broken. How she was empty and has now experienced being replenished. It was when Jesus asked, "Who touched Me?" that she responded by telling her story. Can't you see her in the crowd, afraid and trembling, but still telling her story? Telling how she had depleted all her resources and was still in bondage to her illness. Telling how she had heard that Jesus was near and she determined that it was Jesus who could heal her – completely. Telling how she had to get down to her knees just to touch the hem of His clothing. Telling how, in just a touch, she was made whole and she was healed. Just in a touch, she moved from rock bottom to standing in the midst of a crowd, exclaiming to the world how she had been made whole. Moved from less than to being whole. Moved from being a victim to being victorious. Moved from being an outcast to being in the presence of Jesus, complete and whole.

For us to operate in our greatness (our greatness as determined by our alignment with the will of God), we must openly and freely share with others about the goodness of our God. We must respond to God's instruction to share our victories with others so that He can get the glory. Our testimony matters. Just think about how this woman's testimony touched those that were in the crowd and her testimony continues to touch and transform people today.

Your greater is not for you; it is so that others can see the greatness that is available to them if they align themselves with the Greatest of Greatness! That requires you to open your mouth and share. Sharing the good, the bad, the indifferent and the ugly. We must move from a place of guilt, shame and fear. We must allow God to use us for His glory and to use our stories as an encouragement for others. People must be able to conceptualize the possibilities through our experiences.

T3:

Speak!

PRAYER:

Dear Lord,

I have a testimony and I'm going to tell it. I'm telling so that others can see You in the middle of it all. Help me to tell it and to do so – fearlessly.

In the name of a glorified Jesus,
Amen

RECEIVE, TELL & LIVE

I can't tell you the number of times I've talked myself out of writing this book. Believe me, they have been too numerous to count. And I've used multiple excuses:

1. I'm not good enough.
2. I'm not well known enough.
3. People really don't want to hear what I've got to say.
4. My past is too tainted for people to be able to see their greater through me.
5. My words won't help anyone.
6. I don't want to be embarrassed.
7. This won't help the Kingdom.

Listen, I could list many more reasons why I shouldn't, couldn't and therefore, I wouldn't and I didn't. It was in these spaces that I would remember either Biblical stories, or I would hear a sermon, or I would feel deep down in my soul that I needed to share my very common experience with God so that others, in spite of their present condition, might see themselves in a deep and rewarding relationship with Him.

The woman here, after determining that her replenishment was in her touching or getting into the presence of the One with power and authority to restore and heal her, did three things:

1. She received her healing.
2. She told her story, and
3. She lived in greater.

Look at the verses:

1. In verse 28, she reached up and touched Him.
2. In verse 29, immediately she was healed.
3. In verse 33, she fell to her face, worshipped Him and testified to Him in the presence of the crowd about all that she had gone through and what she had done.
4. In verse 34, Jesus changed her status from the afflicted outcast to the beloved Daughter and invited her to go in peace. To live fully in her healing.

Once you've been made free, the expectation is that you will live fully in your freedom. What does that mean? It means that you will stand confidently in alignment with God's will for your life and you will engage in your calling so that you can glorify Him by embracing your greater.

T3:

Receive your healing, accept your calling and engage in the work.

PRAYER:

Dear Lord,

Use me.

In the engaging name of Jesus,
Amen

REESTABLISH:

TO BRING BACK, TO BE ESTABLISHED AGAIN

The creation of man(woman)kind:
Genesis 1:26 – 31

God's Process for Greatness

Everything that God does, He does it with excellence and in perfection. What I find so amazing is that God, the Being with all authority and power, pauses so that He can admire and evaluate His handiwork, His craftmanship. Every time I read Genesis 1, all I can picture is God sitting back, after each phase of His creation plan, crossing his arms and nodding His head in satisfaction and appreciation of His work. Can't you see it? He steps into nothingness and:

- speaks light into existence, then, with His arms crossed and thinking to Himself, "Now, that's good!" (v. 3);
- speaks the division of the heavens from the earth, "Yep, I did that!" (v. 6);
- speaks the development of the earth as we understand it, "Look at that. Now that's good" (v. 9);
- speaks the vegetation, the fruit, the herbs into existence and develops the method for each to reproduce as He thinks to Himself, "Now this is good!" (v. 11);

- speaks the solar system and the seasons into being and He takes the moment to celebrate the advancement of His plan (v. 14);
- brings life to the birds and to the fish and He marvels at His work, giving it a perfect score (v. 20);
- creates the animals and everything that creeps on the earth, and takes a beat to admire His workmanship (v. 24).

Please don't think that I am trivializing God's work. What I am doing is making it easier for both you and me to see the intentionality of God in the execution of His plan. I don't know if you see it. God has an apparent and well executed plan for the creation of life and everything that supports it. With every step and each progression, I can see the intentionality of God. Nothing is created out of order, and nothing is created without His evaluation and His approval. He made sure that He didn't create fish or cattle or birds of the air before He created the perfect environment that would enable them to survive and to thrive. God, in all of His awesomeness, is so intentional, ensuring that all details are tended to, that His progress is evaluated and that each success is celebrated.

God has given us the process for us to move from nothingness to creation, engagement and completion of somethingness (not sure, but did I just make up a word?). Look at God:

1. Plan
2. Create
3. Evaluate
4. Celebrate

Right there is the outline that each of us can use when we resolve that we are going to step into our God-ordained calling and submit to the process that He has provided – plan, create, evaluate and celebrate. Yes, God intends for us to get to the place where our passions align and collide with our calling and we step into our greater purposefully and boldly. And, He has provided us with the blueprint for success. He created the plan, the process, the pattern so that we could replicate it and live our lives out loud. Living so that He gets the glory and others are attracted to the wonderfulness of having a full, deep and rich relationship with the Father.

T3:

God has provided the process for us to move from nothingness to creation, engagement and completion of somethingness:

- Plan
- Create
- Evaluate
- Celebrate

PRAYER:

Dear Lord,

You are a God of plans and of strategy. You are deliberate. As I desire to be more and more like You, help me to develop a spirit of intentionality.

In the intentional name of Jesus,
Amen

No Limits

I have a friend who has just launched a new career. She confessed that when she was much younger, she had always dreamed of inspiring and supporting others to live their best lives. However, as she got older, and because of multiple life events, disappointments and difficulties, she lost sight of her passion and her vision. She began to think it was going to be too hard and she had waited too long. She could no longer envision herself starting the work to do what she always dreamed of – her passion, her greater. So, she resigned herself to doing everything else. She limited herself because she was focused on what she didn't have rather than being focused on WHO she had. Now, don't get me wrong – she has lived a fruitful and productive life. But she has not lived in the greater – the space that God had crafted and ordained for her to fill.

Recently, she told me that she'd started to dream again. She was beginning to see herself living in her passion. With tears rolling down my face, I encouraged her, I praised God for her responding to the call and I pledged my support. As I hung up the phone, I thought about how I have allowed so many things to stop me from moving into my calling and living the life that God intended. Nothing limited me; I placed limitations on myself! Because she shared, I was inspired to redirect my thinking and recommit to my calling.

Every time I've read Genesis 1, I tend to read it quickly because I think that I fully understand the point: God created the heavens and the earth and everything within... However, recently, I was reading God's word without really having a specific purpose in mind. I was just reading. I was compelled to go back to the beginning, Genesis 1. I decided that I was going to take my time and try to see it from a different angle. I wanted to shift my paradigm. I made sure to allow the words to not only touch my heart, but to penetrate my mind and reshape my thinking. Then I came to verse 28 and it hit me a totally different way: *"Then God blessed them, and said to them, 'Be fruitful and multiply; fill the earth and subdue it; have dominion over the fish of the sea, over the birds of the air, and over every living thing that moves on the earth'"* (Genesis 1:28 NKJV).

God created man/woman and He gave us purpose and power with only one limitation, not to eat from the Tree of Good and Evil. God told us to produce, to create, to subdue, to lead, to operate in our authority, to take our place as He has ordained it. Wow! He gave us purpose! He gave us work! He gave us His expectations! One significate expectation being that we do not eat from the Tree of Good and Evil. But He didn't give us limits. Really, what He gave us wasn't limits but it was expectations along with His permission to live our lives and to live them fully.

We're created to live in greatness. However, we have allowed, because of the difficulties of life, limitations to be placed on our lives. God desires us to live out our ordained purpose, without limits.

We must reshape our thinking and redirect our focus so that we can reestablish His intent for us. We must begin to live in the space of greater!

T3:

God has given us so much. He gave us purpose! He gave us work! He gave us His expectations! But He didn't give us limits. Ultimately, He gave us His permission to live our lives and to live them fully.

Prayer:

Dear Lord,

You have made me a steward of all that You have created. You have given me permission to live a life of purpose and to handle Your business in a manner that meets Your expectations. Strengthen me so that I step into Your business with respect and courage and without fear.

In the gracious name of Jesus,
Amen

GETTING UNSTUCK

I love to travel, and my favorite way of traveling is by car. If you are like me, when traveling by car (of course you aren't the driver at this point), you look around to see what you can see. I'm also sure that you have seen the bumper sticker that says (paraphrasing) "Stuff Happens!" There has never been a truer statement! Regardless of who you are, what you have, what you look like, how educated you are, how gifted and talented you are, how athletic you are, with all your advantages and with all the "things" that have set you up for success, stuff still happens. Even as a Believer, stuff still happens. Difficulties and storms arise, often out of nowhere and without warning, and you find yourself thrown off course and derailed.

When you started your journey, you were walking with confidence in your God-given calling, focused on Jesus and being led by the Spirit. Experiencing wins and enjoying the journey. You were traveling at a good clip and experiencing positive results. Suddenly, stuff happened, and you lost your way and found yourself stuck. Stuck in the madness, stuck in the mess, stuck in discontent, stuck in anger, stuck in guilt and shame, stuck in fear, stuck in being unproductive, unfocused and lost. All of a sudden, Stuck Boulevard has become your home. It is the space that you now occupy and reside, and you've unpacked your bags and decided to stay a while.

The odd thing about Stuck Boulevard is that the longer you stay, the more stuck you become. So much so that you lose sight of where you were going and you forget that you were destined and designed for greater! You begin to develop negative traits and characteristics that resemble all the other residents of Stuck Boulevard. You have no focus, no drive; you're unhappy and sad, having lost your joy, feeling disconnected from the power that once fueled and energized you. God seems so far away. It's quite possible that you don't feel His presence at all. Your light is dim, and the thrill of life is gone. You are existing, but you definitely aren't thriving.

How do we get from where we are to where we need to be – in the space of our greater?! How do we get back on the correct course so that we can find our passion and our joy again?

We must reestablish our commitment and our promise to the authority of our lives. The apostle Paul gives us clear instructions when we feel as if we've lost our way in Philippians 3:12 – 16. In those scriptures, Paul describes that he has a God-given goal that maintains his focus while realizing that he hadn't yet achieved it. He suggests that at times he has endured some challenges that could have potentially derailed him, but he stayed the course. It is during those challenging times that he resolves that he is going to get all that God has for him.

For Believers to get it all, we must press. We must exert some energy, be tenacious and push! We must recalibrate our intentions and focus on Jesus. Paul is forewarning us that even when we are single-minded and focused, we will be required to press. Past the stuff. Press! Enduring the challenges and the difficulties. Press! Ignoring those things that may divert our attention. Press! Moving aside our inclination to indulge in a pity party. Press! Looking above and beyond the haters and the naysayers. Press! Not to concentrate on the pain and the disappointment. Press! When it seems as if the obstacles are bigger than our strength or our power. Press! When we are so exhausted that our tired is tired. Press!

Then Paul encourages us to recalibrate, to refocus and to reestablish in our hearts God's intentions. To do this requires commitment. We must commit to living the greater and getting all that God has appointed for us. Then we must submit to the plan, remain focused and continue to push.

T3:

When we recalibrate, refocus and reestablish, God will, as stated in the Message Bible, *"clear"* our *"blurred vision"* (Philippians 3:16). Then we are expected to get on track and to stay on it!

PRAYER:

Dear Lord,

I want to please You. Help me to press and to push until You are glorified.

In the powerful name of Jesus,
Amen

You're Greater

When I was in high school, I always thought that my school was huge. I felt so small compared to my surroundings. Now, let's be clear, I wasn't small in stature or in build. My feelings of "smallness" were not centered on the building itself, but on all the hustle and bustle that was going on around me. It just seemed as if my classmates were going somewhere that I wasn't. My thoughts, my dreams and my perspective all seemed too small when I compared them to other's. For example, I would hear people talk about their plans for after high school. They all seemed to have plans, and although I knew I was going to college, I had no idea what that meant for me. And I didn't even try to guess how my life would be (or could be) beyond college.

As I matured, I maintained the habit of not thinking greater! I bound my dreams so tightly that I refused to allow them to breathe, to grow. I refused to allow my dreams to see the light of day. Yes, I heard all the pastors and Sunday school teachers who encouraged me and everyone else to see beyond the right now, the mortal. However, there was something within that would not let me dream big. Don't know if it was fear, shame, too many disappointments, too many times of being discouraged. Honestly, I'm not sure.

As a result of my limited, stagnated and tiny thinking, I missed opportunities to hear God and to tap into the plans that He had/ has for me. God was talking, and I was ignoring Him. Quieting His voice so that it met my expectations. Making sure that I didn't allow my mind to take me places that I felt I couldn't reach.

All the while, I was claiming that God didn't want to use me because I wasn't worthy to be used. Now, how crazy is that? If you read just a little of your Bible, you will see that God gets the most out of those that would regularly be looked down upon. Shoot, I've given you plenty of examples already. Women who were seen as less than, but were able to go beyond their present situations and position themselves for the greater that God had for them.

In Colossians 3:2, God speaks to how we should think. He tells us to set our minds on the greater and see beyond limitations and the trivial. If we would just stop concentrating on the things we can see and adjust our Heavenly spectacles onto the things that we can't see, bigger and greater won't seem so impossible.

We must recalibrate our attention and our focus. We must develop Heavenly vision and focus onto Heavenly places. We have got to train our hearts to concentrate on the things above and disregard those things that may discourage us. In order to get to the greater, we have to elevate our gaze and our thoughts. We have to develop an attitude that greater is within and God's intentions for my life ain't small.

Please understand, I know that the process of correcting our tendency to think and to live small is not easy. We have to be intentional in the process. We have to lean into the possibilities that God has outlined for our lives.

T3:

Small ain't my size and it ain't my life! I'm intended for GREATER!

PRAYER:

Father,

You aren't small, and you never wanted me to live a small life. I will remember that greater is the expectation. Keep me focused in spite of what may come against me. Greater is the expectation.

In the great name of Jesus,
Amen

It's Possible

Yep, it's true. Don't rely on the things that you know, or even your past experiences. Hear me when I say that there is a thing that is burning within you, keeping you from staying still and getting rest. That thing that keeps popping up in your being, begging you to pay attention. That thing that has been with you since you can remember, sometimes laying low and being still, but never leaving you. That thing that when you step into it, even if it's momentary, you feel more alive than you've ever felt. That thing that even when you're petrified but you still do it, you are in your most comfortable space. That thing that when you see it in somebody else, you understand it and can relate to it. You gravitate to that thing when you see it in another. Yes, that thing that brings you excitement and joy but makes the butterflies in your stomach to start to flutter – that is your greater! That is your passion and that is your calling. That is your sweet spot!

During the pandemic, my church was forced to hold services virtually, often right from my dining room table. Under normal circumstances, I was the Sunday school teacher for the women's class, and I loved being in that space. Although I love teaching Sunday school, I would shy away from doing it on a larger platform or scale because I never really felt like I was enough. I wasn't smart enough, I didn't know enough to be effective, I didn't have a strong enough vocabulary. I had all kinds of excuses and responses for why I didn't fully step into the space that God had intended for me – my greater. I continuously measured my abilities based on man's standards.

In Mark 10:27, Jesus informed His disciples that getting into Heaven ain't easy if someone tries to enter in under their own power. However, the impossible under man's power is always possible when we plug into the power of Jesus. Yep, not only does that mean that we can get into Heaven, it also means that those Heavenly assignments that God has for our lives – the greater – are also possible. You are absolutely correct: We can't do it. It is impossible, whatever it is. But what we forget is that it is not about us; therefore, it won't be us who makes it happen. We must set our minds on the things above, tap into Jesus' power, commit to the work and watch God be God.

So, here we are more than two years later, and I am still teaching and I have not missed a Sunday. No, not one. I've done whatever was necessary to complete my assignment. If we had to tape a lesson, we've taped it. If I had to do the lesson from a hotel room, we've done it. If we were on vacation, I'd do the lesson and then we would go on with our plans. Nothing has kept me from my assignment. Not only that, but I've also started a ministry, I am writing this book and I am preparing to do even more! This has only happened because I've decided that I want to get to greater! I want to please God. I desire to have God look over the edges of Heaven, see me and smile. He smiles because He is pleased with my service, my obedience and my submission to His will for my life.

Yep, the impossible is made possible by the power of Jesus. That power is made available to us by the love of our Father. That is all!

T3:

Believers must set our minds on the things above, tap into Jesus' power, commit to the work and watch God be God.

PRAYER:

Thank You for being a God that makes the impossible, possible. It is by Your power that I can do anything, especially to live in the greater. I am enough because You are more than enough.

In the name of possibilities, Jesus,
Amen

Going Back is Going Forward

W hat?! What are you saying, going back is going forward?!
Not making sense! It doesn't compute.

I know; when it came to my mind, it didn't make sense to me
either. How's that for transparency? But, once you really think
about it, really allow your mind to wrap itself around the thought,
it becomes clearer.

When we were young, everything in us was about moving
forward. You went from the inability to move on your own, to
crawling, to walking to running. Progress, right? Even in school,
progression is determined by the grade level you have achieved,
and your grade point average determines the level of your success.
Progression, right?

For those of us who have decided we are going to live a life of
abundance, we develop these plans, we have goals and objectives
all for the purpose of moving forward. We refuse to go backwards
because backwards indicates failure and loss. But when we really
begin to understand who God is and how He operates, we begin
to accept the concept of reestablishing ourselves as God intended,

originally! Our joy, our peace and our progression is motivated by our fulfilling the will that God has for us. We must become comfortable with submitting to the process or going back for the purpose of moving forward.

In Genesis 1:26 KJV, God creates man and woman, but the process is much different than when He created the rest of the Heavens and the earth. When He created man, He called the entire Trinity together so they could pour into man everything that is needed on his journey to greatness. Notice God states, *"Let Us make man in Our image, according to Our likeness."* Then in verse 27, after the conversation with God the Son and God the Holy Spirit, it states, *"So God created man in His own image; in the image of God He created him; male and female, He created them."*

When creating man in His image and likeness, God is giving us the ability and the character of perfection and greatness:

- Like God, we can create something out of nothing.
- Like Jesus, we can redeem, restore, move mountains and bring life to what seems dead.
- Like the Holy Spirit, we can show compassion, correct with love and direct others to their greatness.

Our entire life's journey, once we've accepted Jesus as our Lord and Savior, is about our going back in order to go forward. It is about being reestablished in perfection. Yep, you were created in perfection, perfectly created. Our greatness, our next is encapsulated in our willingness to embrace and engage in the journey of getting back to what is already within – perfection!

Be willing to go back to go forward!

T3:

Our greatness, our next is encapsulated in our willingness to embrace and engage in the journey of getting back to what is already within – perfection!

PRAYER:

Father:

Because You are perfect and You created me in Your image and likeness, I have the potential for perfection. I am committed to going back so that I can progress based on Your desires and expectations. Lord, take me back to that place where I am perfect and I bring You pleasure.

In the perfect name of Jesus,
Amen

TRANSFORMATION

The idea of transformation brings to mind an image of someone becoming something other than what they already are. It conjures images of someone being brand new; a new creature; no longer the same. In fact, the Bible tells us that when we accept Jesus, we become new. The definition of transformation states that it is the act or process of changing *completely*. Yep, I totally agree that, as Believers, those of us desiring to move from where we are to our greatness must be transformed – completely. We must discard the old and embrace the new.

However, here's the difficult concept that we must learn: our transformation is not into something that is brand new, something we've never seen or been before. Our transformation is rooted and grounded in how God created us originally: in perfection. We've been in the space of greater before but we were deformed by sin; we are just reestablishing ourselves. Reestablishing ourselves to be truer representatives of who God really is. Doing so by tapping into those aspects of our being that were planted within us by the Trinity during creation.

Remember, in Genesis 1 it states that the Trinity came together and created both male and female. Here's the thing: we were created in their image and in their likeness. We were formed in perfection! (I keep repeating our being created in perfection because we really need to get it!) That ought to excite everything within you. You were created in perfection! If you know our God, you know that there is nothing imperfect in Him. If you understand the Trinity, you understand that there is nothing imperfect within Them. Therefore, if we are made in Their image, having Their abilities and power and in Their likeness, possessing Their character and personality, we too have perfection within.

It is God's desire that we give Him praise. How do we praise Him? By living out His intentions on earth. By living out His love, by stepping into His light and into His power and revealing to the world who He really is. We must step into His will for our lives, endure the trials and the difficulties for the purpose of being reestablished in perfection. Like that famous jarred spaghetti sauce, "it's in there." Perfection is within, and our greater is determined by our willingness to endure the transformative process of trials and tribulations so that we can shed those things that we no longer need to get to those things that validate the greatness of our God.

Yep, your transformation will yield something new. However, your new ain't really new. Your new is grounded in the reestablishment of your original formation – perfection!

T3:

Embrace your perfection! Know that you were perfectly created! Endure the journey and get excited about the "new" you, the transformed you, the greater you!

PRAYER:

Lord,

Help me to get to where I was originally created, in perfection. I am perfectly created because of who You are, and I am thankful.

In the perfect name of Jesus,
Amen

CONCLUSION

Throughout this book I've really been hammering the ideas that every Believer:

- Is created in the image and likeness of God the Father, God the Son and God the Holy Spirit, and since God is perfect, so is the Believer. However, we have to do the transformative work of getting back to what God originally intended.
- Has a God-given calling that will collide with their passion. In this place is where you will find the sweet spot of life. It won't be easy, but it will be abundantly fulfilling.
- Is intended by God to live a life of GREATER! God did not create you, the Believer, to be mediocre, small or limited. The Believer's possibilities are limitless because with God, everything is possible.

Before you close the book, I *need* you to grasp what God really means when He says that He has greater available for you. I truly believe that once you reprogram your mind to accept the fact that your possibilities are endless, you will start to move from a place of fear to living authentically and boldly within your God-given calling.

I am one who was once living small, and, let the truth be known, there are occasions when I shrink back to the familiar. I know how difficult it is to move beyond the feelings of lack and of not being enough. For whatever reasons, possibly because of the multiple negative and disheartening experiences that we've encountered, the concept of greater can escape us. Greater just seems to be out of our reach. I get it. However, it is vitally important that we work desperately to reshape our minds and reposition the paradigm that we look through. For us to live a life that is pleasing to God where we have joy, peace and a whole lot of happiness, we must accept that we are perfectly created and, therefore, we are enough. We have enough for God to effectively use us in His plan. Especially when we know that He doesn't have to use us for anything, but He chooses to do so. Our God majors in the impossible, and He uses us so that the world can see His greatness and His love.

During the last meal that Jesus shared with the disciples before He is betrayed by Judas, taken from courtroom to courtroom, led to the cross where He dies for the atonement of our sins, rises from the dead, returns to the disciples and ascends into Heaven so that He can sit at the right hand of the Father to advocate for you and me, Jesus instructs the Disciples about their GREATER! . Bam! Right there! Jesus informs them that what they've seen is nothing compared to what they will be empowered to do! In John 14:12 – 14, Jesus gives three assurances for the Believer:

- They will be able to do the works that Jesus has done,
- They will do GREATER works than what Jesus had done, and
- If they ask for something in the name of Jesus, He will do it so that His Father will be glorified.

Please, Friend, take a moment to read the verses for yourself. When you reach the word GREATER, stop reading! Take a deep breath and read it again. Pause and meditate on what Jesus just told the disciples. If they – if we – have faith and we pattern our lives after the perfect life of Jesus, GREATER is in their – in our – future. In fact, Jesus said that if we ask for the greater in the precious name of Jesus, God will assuredly answer the prayer.

Now, I need to add that GREATER, here, does not mean bigger or more significant. Rather, it means that by the sheer number of people engaged in their callings and pressing toward the continual transformation to where they are attempting to attain the perfection that is within, we will be able to touch more lives and provide more opportunities for people to witness the love, power and authority of our Father, the creative God, the God of greater.

I hope you are running like I am. I pray that you are experiencing a level of excitement that is difficult to contain. I hope you have shifted the paradigm that you view your possibilities through. I hope your self-perception has positively shifted. I desire that you have experienced a:

- Redesignation of your self-image
- Realignment of your focus
- Redirection of your thinking

- Redefinition of your character
- Revival of your calling
- Replenishment of your courage, and
- Reestablishment of your belief in your being perfectly created.

Friend, you are capable of more, of greater and of moving to the next. I thank God that He has allowed me the opportunity to be a part of your journey, and I am anticipating the testimonies that you will share about what God is doing through you.

I pray that you better understand why I started with calling you friend. I hope you include me on your list as someone who will lift you up and pour positively into your life. I pray you also understand that I am willing to shine the light into some dark spaces so you can begin the work of change and transformation. I am also here so you can share the victories, the challenges and the testimonies of your journey. We are in this thing together.

I am blessed by this experience, and I pray you, too, are blessed!

T3:

> *"Most assuredly, I say to you, he who believes in Me, the works that I do he will do also; and GREATER works than these he will do..."* John 14:12 NKJV (emphasis mine).

PRAYER:

Holy Father,

Guide me, and I will follow. I will follow You to my GREATER so You will be glorified through me.

In the greater and perfect name of Jesus,

Amen, amen and amen!